"10 Things Every Black Man Should Know."

THE URGENCY OF KNOWING

Dr. Marrix D. Seymore Sr.

Rackhouse Publishing

Read to Learn, Write to Remember

References

1. Bates, K. G., Hudson, K. E. (2006). The New Basic Black: Home Training for Modern Times. United States: Doubleday.
2. Black Lives. (2020). Blacklivesmatter.com
3. Carson, R. (2009). Taming Your Gremlin (Revised Edition): A Surprisingly Simple Method for Getting Out of Your Own Way. United States: William Morrow Paperbacks.
4. Claro, S., Paunesku, D., and Dweck, C. (2016). "Growth mindset tempers the effects of poverty on academic achievement," PNAS 113 (31) 8664-8668; first published July 18, 2016; https://doi.org/10.1073/pnas.1608207113
5. Harrison-Hale, A. (2002) "Conflict Resolution Styles Among African Americans," Black Children: Social, educational, and parental environments, 2, 4-19
6. Howe & Lisi. (2018). "Becoming a Multicultural Educator: Developing Awareness, Gaining Skills, and Taking Actions, Sage Publications
7. HR Madhubuti. (2002). "Tough Notes: A Healing Call for Creating Exceptional Black Men: Affirmations, Meditations, Readings, and Strategies," Third World Press
8. Motley, R., & Banks, A. (2018). Black Males, Trauma, and Mental Health Service Use: A Systematic Review. Perspectives on social work : the journal of the doctoral students of the University of Houston Graduate School of Social Work, 14(1), 4–19.
9. Page, L. F., Davis, S., Jenkins, G., Hunt, R. (2003). The Pact: Three Young Men Make a Promise and Fulfill a Dream. United Kingdom: Riverhead Books.
10. Reasons. (2018). 5 Reasons Why Travel is Good for Your Mental Health," Forbes, January 2018
11. Test. (2019). TEST: Do you know your own worth? https://www.psychologies.co.uk/tests/do-you-know-your-own-worth.html
12. Woodward, M. (2017). The psychology of first impression; three tips for making a good one. Psychology Today.

ISBN-13: 978-1-7355350-2-9

For information about custom editions, special sales, premium and bulk purchases, please contact:
WWW.DRSEYMORE.COM

First Edition
Printed in the U.S.A

CONTENTS

DEDICATION & ACKNOWLEDGMENTS

This reflection of life lessons is dedicated to my ancestors of whom I am their wildest dreams and the manifestation of their legacies. Because of L. G. Seymore's "Son, give those books hell," Nolan Williams' "That's my boy," Kenneth Bernard Green's "You still holding your color?" and the brotherhood of Seymore men, I have been compelled to trust God for the plan He still has for my life.

More importantly, this map is dedicated to my seeds. Marrix II and Johnston Alexander Seymore, you have always been my "why." When your mother and I named you, the intentionality of our prayers was for you to spend the rest of your lives thriving as men of honor, distinction, humility, integrity, but most affectionately, as men of God. Know that your family is the most important thing, but even when you have to leave family behind, never leave God. In fact, dwell in His shelter. Make Him your refuge.
Your great grandmother, Nora Seymore, always whispered to me, "You're supposed to see through muddied waters!" Your grandmother, Mary Seymore-Walker said, "I didn't raise any fools!" Those words were their way of setting the standard; making their expectations of me known, and casting vision for my life.

Big shoes were placed at my feet to fill. I am placing my shoes at your feet, not to fill but to grow into your own. Though you both accepted Christ as your Savior at very early ages, I pray that God will constantly remind you that it is through Him, all of your life's aspirations are possible. I believe in you both and if you constantly seek God and His purpose for your lives, I promise you will learn to get past the small stuff and conquer giants.

I

INTRODUCTION
"THE URGENCY OF KNOWING"

"...there is enormous and abundant power in knowing."
-Dr. Marrix D. Seymore Sr.

It was not my intention to talk about the pains and struggles of my life. Instead, this book was supposed to be a single 10-point quick, "read and move on." But when asked the question of how a black boy from 5th Ward Texas, born in the late sixties who had to wear corduroy in the summer earned a PhD, the only way to appropriately respond was to first, unpack my own life experiences. It would be those experiences that would not only teach me how to survive, but also how to surpass the odds that had been stacked against me.

When I first attempted to write, I had accepted a position as a Professor of Education at Lincoln University in Jefferson City, Missouri. I was also the Director of a Black Male Teacher Initiative. Part of my responsibility was to shore up the institution's attempt to increase the graduation rate of Black males who majored in Education. From that effort, I founded the Academy for Male of Color in Education. Through the ivy brick gates of "Lincoln O Lincoln," I brought with me the experiences as a father of two amazing sons and a rewarding career as a public school educator and administrator. I had been afforded the opportunity to be a successful pastor and national trainer who had attained a Bachelor of Science Degree in Education, a Master of Education Degree, and a Doctorate of Philosophy. The lessons I learned through the work of mentoring 50 young men majoring in Education, as well as other majors, quickly confirmed why I transitioned from traditional pastoral ministry to what I like to call, "ministry in the market place."

At the conclusion of that first year, I began to organize the initial themes of what I had come to understand about "knowing." Man! When I think about some of the decisions I have made, I ask, "Why did I say or do that?" Many of the young men I have had the honor of engaging with have said or done things that did not always turn out well. They have responded to situations in ways which did more damage to their self-image and reputations than they anticipated.

When I think of choices many young men of my village and other communities make today, I have often found myself asking, "Why didn't that young man do something this way, or that way?" "Didn't he know better?" The truth of the matter is, when a young man makes a not-so-great decision, it isn't because he does not have the right intention. Dr. C. Gould once told me, "Impact and intent are different." In many instances, he simply doesn't know any better. Many guys just don't have the right information to make the best decisions at a given time. As a result, some of them could have developed negative perceptions about themselves, about other people, and the world around them. Such a tainted outlook could have eventually consumed them with doubt, fear, and even anger, had they not been taught what to say in certain situations and how to respond to others.

Each time I sat to write, I kept seeing my own life in each theme, but never considered myself as an example. When I felt like the outline was complete, I could not ignore the flood of memories that were now at the forefront of my every thought. I still resisted the very thought of sharing my past in a book. Maybe I felt too much would be exposed. Maybe I was ashamed. Let me be clear; I wasn't ashamed that my past was painful. I was in some way, not counting my past as a building block to who and what I am today. That was the shameful part. Besides, who wanted to read about another Black boy from the hood?

But when I thought about the rich culture I am a part of and how to "be" was passed down from one generation to another, regardless of the situation; when I think about all the Black boys from marginalized communities like mine, constantly being penalized for what they don't know, couching my experiences in a few lines and points went from a pressing idea to a duty and an urgent responsibility.

There is a tribe of East Africans who live in southern Kenya and northern Tanzania called the Maasai. The Maasai was known for their fierce warriors who were mighty in battle and feared by all other tribes. To be a well-respected Maasai warrior was a big deal. All the young males of the village spent their boyhood watching and imitating the men in hopes one day they too would become a warrior. In order to become a warrior, a young adult male not only had to be disciplined, mature, fast, and skilled with a weapon, but he would also have to go out into the wild, often with just a spear, to kill a lion, bringing its head back to the tribal leaders as proof. You can probably figure out that if the boy didn't kill the lion, the lion killed the boy. Those young men who made it back with the head of a lion were then raised as a warrior. The young warrior then wore the lion's head as a sort of crown or badge of honor.

When Maasai warriors met each other, there was a traditional greeting that translated to mean, "And how are the children?" In the native tongue, the traditional response was, "And all the children are well." When a warrior responded that all the children were well, he was respectfully acknowledging to fellow warriors that he himself had assumed his duty in the village.

He was also saying that he had done all he could do to make sure the elderly, the young, and the fatherless were safe.

At some point, despite the need to protect myself from the social microscope; putting aside several thoughts of aborting this project again, I assumed my responsibility to the village. A story of fear and trembling, a record of self-acceptance, a healing letter of "stumble, fall, get up, press repeat" has now landed in print.

There are some essentials that every man of color needs to know to function and contribute to the world at his optimal best. He must revisit those elements throughout his life until he has mastered being his optimal self. The Urgency of Knowing is a retooling and revamping, rethinking and reimagining our way of mastering everything as we grow.

In this book, I want to share with you a lifetime of information that I feel is urgent to your success as a young man, especially one of color. Let's be clear, I am not attempting to dictate what you should do.

That goes against the village principle of respecting a fellow warrior. It doesn't matter what path you take in life. You may become a surgeon, artist, engineer, teacher and yes, the President of the United States. I want you to KNOW that you have "IT!"

My intent, however, is to equip your mind, expose your heart, and engage your spirit with basic knowledge that will help you make more informed decisions for yourself at any given time. I want to make sure you know what you need to know before you have to use it. What you, as a young men of color, don't know can and will limit the potential-who and what you can become. Let me be clear. I am an educator with experiences as a Black man, speaking to Black men. However, I realize that issues that I have had to deal with like racism, discrimination, colorism/"otherism," other males of color also have had to deal with them as well. My hope is to use my experiences to empower all men of color.

1

KNOW HOW TO CONTROL YOUR MIND

"I am no less a man because I fear. I am no less a man because of mental health struggles. I am no less a man because only I get to decide what it means for me to be a man".
-Shawn Henfling

Emotional Rollercoasters

It's hard to not be an angry Black man in America, or any other place in the world for that matter. We are constantly riding on social rollercoasters. Every day, society dictates a narrative about us that never depicts who we truly are. We're also riding spiritual rollercoasters. Many days, it is a difficulty to believe in God, the universe, or even ourselves. We are always riding emotional rollercoasters but despite that, many of us start each new day wearing a mask to cover the true feelings we battle inside.

One morning, as I was preparing to go to work, my phone rang. I was caught off guard. Most who know me, know I am not a morning person, nor do I like talking on the phone. So the phone ringing that early meant one thing-an emergency! My mind immediately when into panic mode. When I looked at the caller ID, a friend's name popped up that I hadn't talked to in quite some time. We text and send instant messages via Facebook every now and then, inquiring about family and children, but we hardly ever talk on the phone, especially that early. After all, he's an educator, like me, he should have been preparing to meet his students. Why was he calling me?

When I answered the phone, my friend and I went through the usual exchange, "Hey man," "What's up," etc. I then accelerated the conversation with, "Why are you not in class?" He responded with a series of strange questions that ended with "How did you get through it?" His voice was trembling. It became clear my friend was having marital problems and was, in a "manly way," asking for help. As he explained bits and pieces of his situation, it was clear what he needed to say: "I don't know what to do."

I suddenly felt like I was at the start of a familiar rollercoaster and it was revving its engine all over again. I could sense the fear and panic in his voice. There were long pauses. I recognized the overwhelming sensation of being on the brink of losing everything. He had a budding career, a beautiful wife, and two amazing sons. He was living the dream with a family in the suburbs, a two-story house, a white picket fence, and a dog.

Nearly 20 years ago, I went through the same thing. At the time, I panicked. I was in a tough situation and I had no idea what to do. When I thought life was on a high, a sharp, lightning-fast dip came, just like a rollercoaster.

Unfortunately, my rollercoaster ended in divorce. As we talked, my friend continued to explain, but with each word, my heart rate rose. Between the conflicting emotions stirring within me, I wondered, "Why is he asking me about this?" "God what do I say?" "How did I feel back then?" "C'mon Seymore, how did you handle your situation?"

During that time, I was all over the place. Each day, I went from anger to disappointment, on to confusion, and straight into despair. Every time I thought about the things that were going on, I'd get so angry that I would see nothing but blackness. I called that my "black wall experience." When I could think straight, I would examine and cross-examine myself as if I had single-handedly committed a crime. I persecuted myself for everything that could have contributed to my current situation. Everything I thought was negative and destructive.

During the conversation with my friend, I wanted to rush in and save the day, but I remembered when I was in that same emotional place, I called one of my friends. I tried to remember how he supported me.

Sidebar: never underestimate the value of someone else's experiences. We go through the craziest things in life and somehow come out in a better place. Our experiences become lessons not only for ourselves, but also for others. There is always another brother setting his life by yours; saying to himself, "If he can handle that, I can handle this." It is important to search for the lesson in every rollercoaster event.

Back then, the friend that I reached out to did not attempt to save the day. He knew I suffered from atrial fabulation-irregular heartbeat due to stress. So the first point of order was to get my emotions under control. My friend allowed me to be in pain, to be hurt and angry and disappointed without giving me instructions. In other words, he let me feel. Picture this man, standing outside a locker room watching the door as I cried, screamed, and yelled my heartache, without anyone ever knowing.

As days went by, I began to prioritize the things I could change or handle. It was all I could focus on. Anything I could not change did not make it to the agenda. I remember hearing him say, "You have to take care of your sons. You need your job to do that. If your emotions interfere with your work, you lose your job. If you lose your job, you cannot take care of your sons."

In the middle of the emotional rollercoaster ride of divorce, I had a wakeup call. If I had not gotten a grip on the way I was thinking at that time, my story could have gone so many other, negative ways. Because of my own experience and the support I received, I knew I had to help my friend. On the other end of that morning's call was a brother riding an emotional roller coaster. He needed help. He needed a confidant to respect his manhood, but also stand outside the locker room. He needed to make a shift in his thinking in that moment.

Do You Know How To Reset Your Mind?

Every Black man needs to know how to reset his mind, how to flip the switch toward a new mindset. He needs to know how to reframe his perspective of himself. A person's usual attitude or mental state is his or her mindset[4]. It influences our decisions, choices, attitudes, behaviors and lifestyle. Some mindsets are fixed, meaning the thinking is "this is the way things have always been and will always be this way. Things will never change." Therefore, no effort is put forth to change. There is also a growth mindset, meaning that there is always room for change, growth, and improvement. A person with a growth mindset seeks ways to improve themselves or achieve more. Sometimes, a mindset has the power to spread between people in a group and influences the entire group's outlook.

Black men throughout history have overcome monumental challenges in their lives and have done so with their heads held high. Their resilience and tenacity were the manifestation of their mindsets. When you know how to reset your mindset, you control the outcome. When you don't, the outcome controls you. If you are angry and lash out at someone, the outcome is usually something you live to regret. There is a biblical philosophy, "So as a man thinks, so is he." Black men must be able to reimagine how they see themselves and envision their potential from an "I can" frame of mind: such changes start in the mind.

One way to reset your mind is to stop speaking negatively about yourself. It is so easy to think that you are the only man dealing with problems. In fact, everyone else is too. One of those problems is dealing with trauma. In America, every Black man has directly or indirectly suffered some form of trauma. Trauma shapes our minds. Studies examining trauma exposure among community samples of Black males show that approximately 62% have directly experienced a traumatic event in their lifetime, 72% witnessed a traumatic event, and 59% have learned of a traumatic event involving a friend or family member[8].

Do you know how to identify and overcome Trauma?

Trauma is the response to a deeply distressing or disturbing event that overwhelms our individual ability to cope. It causes feelings of helplessness, diminishes our sense of self, and our ability to feel the full range of emotions and experiences. Trauma can be a specific stressful event that causes psychological damage. That's called acute trauma. Repeated and prolonged exposure to stressful events that influence our mental state are also forms of trauma-chronic trauma. Exposure to multiple stressful events that negatively forms our perspective is trauma. For example, child abuse, once or ongoing, personally or of someone else, is a traumatic experience. Such exposure is considered to be complex trauma.

Black males experience historical trauma, or intergenerational trauma. This type of trauma is caused by events that target a group of people. Family members who have not directly experienced the trauma can feel the effects of the event generations later. Black males also have Post Traumatic Slave Syndrome (PTSS), a condition that exists as a consequence of centuries of chattel slavery, followed by institutionalized racism and oppression. PTSS has resulted in multigenerational adaptive behavior in Black males, some positive that reflect resilience, and others which are harmful and destructive. Being bullied once or over time is a form of trauma. Witnessing someone being beat up causes trauma. Being denied opportunities like going to a certain school or living in a certain neighborhood because of your racial identity is considered a form of trauma. It leaves you feeling overwhelmed and isolated. That sense of helplessness shapes how you think. Trauma can lead to stress, depression, and substance abuse.

There is no cure for trauma, nor any quick fixes for the suffering associated with them. However, there are some things you can do right now. First, minimize the negative information you consume on social media and television. Then, set some boundaries around what you will and will not talk about, especially if the endgame is not to heal from the conversation. Finally, lean on friends, family, and mental health professionals for support. There is no shame in asking, "what do I do?"

Do You Know what triggers you?

Your mindset can also be reset by embracing challenges. Problems, obstacles, difficulties, and challenges are those uncontrollable challenges that, oddly enough, guide us to better ourselves. One of the challenges we face is how we cope with trauma. Trauma can have devastating effects on a Black man's emotions, ability to think, learn, and concentrate. It impacts impulse control, self-image, and relationships with others. Trauma creates challenges-emotional triggers. Emotional triggers are words or behaviors in our minds that make us uncomfortable and set off an emotional reaction. For example, someone asking you about personal information could be an emotional trigger. Conversations about how you spend your money might be a trigger. Being stereotyped or racially profiled by someone of another ethnic group might be a trigger. These common triggers evoke emotions of anger, sadness, frustration, etc. In some instances, when we hear, see or experience them, we respond by emotionally withdrawing and/or simply feeling hurt or angry. Some would call that suffering in silence. In other instances, we lash out aggressively, most likely in ways we later regret.

At the time this book was written, the COVID-19 pandemic and social injustices of police brutality on Black males were everyday triggers for Black males. Many of us are frustrated, angry, and feeling left without a way to handle how we feel. How you manage your emotions plays a vital role in your success at work, at home, and in your community.

Personal Application

Identify the top three emotional triggers which cause you to be most upset and where they come from. Create some affirmations that are the opposite of your triggers. Then, whatever you are affirming, act it out every day.

Black men experience trauma and manage the triggers it has created. It is important to reset our mindset. Resetting mindset is intentionally and consciously changing the way we think about ourselves in our current situations

Black men find themselves in headspaces that have either motivated them to move forward or have paralyzed them and they've just learned coping mechanisms, rather than strategies for living. Many of us have traumatic experiences we don't know how to handle. When I was on my emotional roller coaster, I needed help. I could not perfectly articulate what I was feeling. But I knew that I didn't like the way I was feeling. In that moment, I had to make a mental shift, not only for myself, but also for my children and the brothers who, at the time, I didn't know were watching. If we are not careful, the roller coaster of life can lead us toward unhealthy behaviors, ultimately hurting ourselves and those we love, unless we shift our mindset.

But imagine if you could use those ups and downs for good, to improve your life. Imagine reversing the direction of the ride so it leads to a healthier mindset, ultimately uplifting ourselves and the ones who come into contact with us. Changing mindset has to be intentional and deliberate. You don't wait until the emotional triggers are pulled. You have to learn to go ahead and be on the lookout for them. A journey toward your happiness, well-being, and sense of self are worth every moment of your time.

Fix your thoughts on what is true, and honorable, and right and pure, and lovely, and admirable. Think about things that are excellent and worthy of praise." (Philippians 4:8)

2

KNOW WHO YOU ARE

"We, today, stand on the shoulders of our predecessors who have gone before us. We, as their successors, must catch the torch of freedom and liberty passed on to us by our ancestors. We cannot lose in this battle."
- Dr. Benjamin E. Mays

Standing On Broad Shoulders

As far back as I can remember, the "model" American family consisted of a father, mother, and two children. In this family model, fathers told their sons how to be men and showed them by example. Growing up, I didn't have the privilege of knowing and learning from my biological father. However, my community was full of examples of strong men: my grandfather and neighbors, my church pastor and deacons; my uncles, and many more. The two most significant men in my life were my grandfather, Mr. L. G. Seymore; affectionately known as "Big Daddy," and my "Pawran" (Creole title for godfather), Mr. Nolan Joe Williams. Sidebar: my grandfather was only about 5'4'. I could look at the top of his head when standing next to him, but my godfather was at least 6'4". I always had to wait until he sat down to look him in the eyes. These men were stern, yet fair. They had big, attractive personalities, drawing all types of people to them. People always wanted to be around them. Both were men who demonstrated unconditional love for God, their families, and their communities. Both taught me the value of keeping a good name, the importance of keeping my word, the necessity of a good work ethic, and the cruel reality of suffering the consequences of making bad choices.

While my grandfather and godfather were teaching me about changing a tire, building a shed, picking a good watch, or shining a pair of shoes, they never spoke against my biological father. Instead, they helped me develop a sense of purpose and responsibility in the world, despite the absence of the man who gave me life. When shadowing my grandfather at his gas station and auto repair garage, I grew envious of his effortless service to others. On ride-along's with my godfather as he traveled to counsel at drug rehabilitation centers, I developed a desire to become a change agent in the world. Today, I realize I stand on the shoulders of great men like these.

In his book, Tough Notes: A Healing Call for Creating Exceptional Black Men, Haki R. Madhubuti posed the question that all Black men should ask themselves, "Who am I?"[7]

I realize I am all those things my grandfather and godfather poured into me. I developed a passion for serving my community. I became a mentor to youth and continue to work to be a role model for those who do not have dependable men in their lives. I am who I am because I stood on the shoulders of great men like my grandfather and my godfather. They knew who they were. Their service to my life was not just an act, it was an example of how my life should be demonstrated to others.

Dr. Benjamin E. Mays was the former president of Morehouse College, the only all-male, historically Black institution of higher education in the United States. His unique experience in this position led him to remind us that we "stand on the shoulders of our predecessors."

These are not literal shoulders but historical ones, representing the foundation laid for present and future generations by abolitionists, civil rights leaders, pastors, and teachers. They positioned others like you and me to achieve greatness. We all have shoulders to stand on; thus, we have a right and responsibility to live, learn, and achieve what our ancestors could not during their time.

Do You Know Who You Are?

Every young man of color needs to know who he is. He needs to know that he is the product of greatness and that he is great. The downplay of cultural identity and the emphasis on monoculturalism-one way of thinking, feeling, believing, and valuing, might send the message that young men of color do not need to be fully aware of the influence of culture on their lives.

The problem today is when you ask many men to tell you who they are, they most likely tell you their name. While a name does indeed carry power, it does not convey the totality of their being. Knowledge of self increases the value of the name given to them. Some young, black men don't really know who they are. Others are not confident in who they are. When you don't have a true sense of what makes you uniquely you, it is easy to be fooled into believing what the news, social media, and others say about the real you. However, when you know who you are, you can (and will) make a true difference in the world.

I may not know you personally, but I can provide the key components to obtain knowledge of self. We will start with ancestral heritage, then move to your cultural heritage, and end with your legacy, which makes you who you are.

I challenge you to answer the questions along the way. I am confident by the end of the chapter you will be closer to a full awareness of who you are.

Do You Know Where You Come From?

Your ancestral heritage makes you who you are. Ancestral heritage is the unique something about you which comes from those related to you long ago. For example, your handsome face people see first; your brilliant mind that blows them away; the courage you demonstrate every day; all these traits and characteristics have come from your grandparents, their grandparents and so on, all the way back to the beginning of time. You inherited intelligence, creativity, endurance, and faith from your ancestors. What you have inherited from your ancestors makes you who you are and who you will continue to become.

There is an African proverb that says, "Even though a cat goes to a monastery, he is still a cat." This implies that no matter how far you may go from where you started, you take with you the core of who you are. A cat is cat wherever, it goes; that's how ancestry works.

I remember my grandfather saying, "Wherever you go, you take my name. Don't forget that." While most hold that ancestors are those whom you descended from (parents, grandparents, great-grandparents, and so forth), ancestors can take on many other labels. Some ancestors were coaches who stuck with you through pivotal years; others were neighbors that watched you while your parents worked. Whatever form they take; ancestors are part of the reason why you are great.

Growing up, I attended my mother's middle-high school. I soon discovered that I wasn't just going to the school she attended, I was going to be taught by many of the same teachers that taught her. There was Ms. Louis J. Bailey, saying, "Seymore, I taught your mother. I knew what was expected of her, and I know what's expected of you. Don't let me down." Mr. A. W. Williams, who taught most of my family Algebra, pointed long fingers at me and said, "Seymore, I still know how to contact your grandfather at the gas station. He's a hardworking man. You have big shoes to fill." Mrs. Blanche Harding was known by all for saying, "You're rocking the boat. It's going to sail without you!" She told me almost every day, "young man, no matter where you go, you take your family with you. Don't ruin their good name." These teachers reminded me then and continue to remind me why a good reputation is so important.

Sometimes I despised being known by my family ties. I heard about my family at school, at church, and all over the community. That doesn't mean that my family members were all saintly, Ivy League grads who ate with golden spoons. They had their problems too.

However, I realized a standard had been established and my identity had been planted long before I was born. By knowing my ancestral heritage, I better understand why I do the things I do. I also understand why I do them with the level of passion I infuse in the world today. I've lived all over the country and have been a part of some amazing organizations. I've added a few letters behind my name. At the end of the day, I am who I am because of those who came before me.

Whether you grew up with both parents, were raised in foster care, were adopted, or grew up with other family members or friends, don't miss this point. Your ancestry shapes who you are. It gives you a solid head start, providing standards that help guide you along your life's path towards purpose. Just as my family's decisions, successes, challenges and more helped create a framework for my life, your life is a path that your ancestors helped to pave.

No matter how much money you possess, you start ahead, because those who came before you set you up for a greater life than they could know. You can build from there. I appreciate my ancestors and am proud to say: "I'm a Seymore."

Do you know your culture?

Cultural history is a combination of traditions and experiences that over time, define you. It may also connect you to people who share the same values and beliefs. Your culture contributes greatly to your mindset and identity; understanding your culture is paramount to discovering and truly embracing who you are.

When I was much younger, one of my nicknames was "Black." Unlike most babies that are born pink and eventually "turn colors," I was born dark-skinned already, so I was given the nickname, "Black." Back then, I didn't give any thought to the name, other than a term of endearment.

My grandfather was the only other family member that was dark-skinned like me. Everyone else; mother, sister, cousins, uncles, were considered "light-skinned." Any time my grandfather referred to me as "his black grandson," a burst of unbridled pride unleashed within me. In fact, anything he said made me happy: little did I know there was history in my nickname.

My grandfather wasn't nonchalantly calling me "Black" just to make me feel proud. He was intentional, instilling in me the idea that being different was a good thing. For him, being the only dark-skinned child was a different experience when he was young. The culture he grew up in frowned upon being dark. There was a difference in the way people of a darker hue were treated, even among some Black families.

According to the story passed down by my grandfather, his mother, my great-grandmother, grew up with her sisters and their grandmother. As a young girl, she was treated differently because she was darker; she was the "black" daughter. According to the oral history, when her sisters became adults, they abandoned her. Growing up, I never heard any conversations about them.

Similar to my great-grandmother, my grandfather was the only dark child and was treated poorly by his father. In fact, according to my grandmother, my great-grandparents divorced because of my great-grandfather's feelings toward his different, dark son, my grandfather.

In a new blended family, an unshakable sense of pride was instilled in my grandfather, even when others tried to refute it. He was taught to be strong, to see his difference as a gift, not a deficiency. My grandfather was a short man in statue, but his love for life was infectious. When he walked into a room, everyone knew it. If he was telling this story, he'd probably say his self-image is what attracted the young ladies in his town. My grandfather embraced his differences, despite the challenges of being a Black man in his day. It seemed to me that what he had been taught emboldened him to be a stronger role model to many young men in our community.

With the insistence of my grandfather, and how he modeled overcoming the "challenges of being dark-skinned", I grew up accepting my dark skin as something unique. In fact, between he and my grandmother, I was pushed to excel despite what others expected of me. Knowing my grandfather's story gave me strength, focus, and a fierce determination to be a successful, no matter what.

Do you know your Legacy?

Your legacy makes you who you are. Your legacy is a pattern of the large and small actions people remember about you and how it made a difference in their lives and the lives of others. Think of things like volunteering at the community center every Saturday, mentoring boys without male role models, or starting a scholarship fund to make a positive impact on the lives of others. You inherited a legacy from your family and your legacy is what you will be known for. People will remember the things you do in service to others; that's what makes you who you are and who you will continue to become.

While teaching elementary school, I did a lesson on future goals and plans. Most students said they wanted to attend college, join the military, or become civil service workers. Those responses were not unusual, as the school heavily emphasized those types of career plans (even at the elementary school level).

I will never forget one particular student's response when it was his turn to share his plan. To my surprise, he said he would probably go to jail. Naturally, I was shocked.

I waited until after the discussion to pull him aside to discuss his answer. I asked what led him to an inevitable incarceration; his response was heart-wrenching. He responded that since all of his older brothers were in jail, he would end up there as well. Even more disturbing, he told me many people in his home and community reinforced this idea with similar statements.

My impression of this young man was very different. He was a straight- "A" student who could think critically. He could help other students understand where they were making mathematical mistakes. He spoke well. He wrote well. Yet, his family only saw negative possibilities in his future, despite an uncle who was a teacher and a grandfather who was a firefighter. He chose to focus on the pain and heartbreak of his brothers' mistakes, believing his life's path would be a carbon copy of theirs, rather than adopting an attitude of optimism. His thoughts were limiting his legacy. Before he could ever achieve real greatness, he allowed his fears to stop him from even taking the first steps.

Yes, he had good grades, but taking the steps toward success and being confident enough to step into that success are two different things. A person can go to school to become a lawyer, graduate with honors, and never take the bar exam to get the credentials to practice as a lawyer.

As a teacher, I've seen students drop out of school in their senior year. They were so close to their next step, but their inner demons, (fear, doubt, anxiety, etc.) told them to give up and expect the worst outcome for their lives.

My former student couldn't see that we all have members of our families who have made poor decisions in life. We also have others who have made wise choices and overcome challenges to achieve more for those they love. While I have had students go on to be writers, lawyers, architects and teachers, I never heard from this one student again. Although I never heard from him again, I hope he recognized that despite his brother's mistakes, he had the broad shoulders of men like his uncle and grandfather to stand upon.

Know who you are!

You are great because your ancestors were great. We are the sum of both good and bad traits. That is not limiting; it is empowering. "I am a descendent of a whole bunch of folk who couldn't be broken," said Darnell Lamar Walker.

You are intelligent. You are courageous. You are the epitome of greatness. Your ancestral heritage, your cultural history, and your legacy make you who you are and what you will continue to be come.

Know who you are. When you don't know who you are, it is easy to believe what someone else says about you.

Personal Application

Have a conversation with someone who knows your family very well. Ask them where your family came from and go as far back as possible. Ask what the members of your family looked like? What did they do for a living? How did they carry themselves?

Then, ask them what events made your family gather together? Holidays? Special events? Ask about the ways they behaved when they were together? Were they serious? Was their laughter? Ask, what do the people who lived around them remember most about your family? Were there good memories or perhaps, sad or unhappy memories? If so, what happened? Finally, take a moment to reflect on what you learned about your family. Does any of what you heard seem familiar? If so, what? You are who you are because of your ancestry, your culture, and your legacy.

3

KNOW WHEN TO STAND UP & WHEN TO STAND DOWN

*"Ignorance, aligned with power is the most
ferocious enemy justice can have."*
-James Baldwin

The Power of Self-Control

While completing this project, I experienced social, emotional, and physical challenges like never before. More than ever, I had to lean on my experience to know when to stand up…and when to unclench my fists and stand down.

One particular experience sticks out the most; a situation where I had to speak to a staffer to correct unprofessional behavior. I'd been pointing the same issue out for quite some time, but this time, I needed to be direct.

When I raised the issue, the staffer became very annoyed, so much so, they raised their voice to me. In that moment, I felt my heart racing. A small "something" within me, that I'd been able to keep at bay for a long time, was eager to come up, and out. I sat in my seat as the room felt like it was spinning. My focus was fixed on self-control and I felt myself clinching my jaws to maintain a neutral facial expression. I was ready to send this person packing, never to return.

I recognized the moment they knew they'd stepped too far when they immediately asked for the rest of the day off. I thought to myself, "Here's my "way out" of saying the wrong thing." Recognizing the opportunity, I calmly approved the request and let the staffer leave.

The interaction bothered me for the rest of the day and the next morning. If only he had practiced restraint, the interaction could have gone another way. As his superior, I knew he was not within his rights to speak to me that way. I also knew it was my responsibility to stand down and keep my personal feelings out of the professional world. I remembered a principal mentor of mine and how he handled situations that had been blown overboard. I remember my pastor and how he would always aim to calm a situation, rather than allow things to be said that could not be taken back. It was what I learned from their example that influenced how I handled this situation. In this moment, being right was not the objective-it was to control myself.

In this chapter, you will come to know how rights, responsibilities, and respect influence how you respond to the rollercoasters of your particular life. A clear understanding of the three components will guide you in knowing when to stand up…and when to stand down.

Know your Rights?

The first component to knowing when to stand up…and when to stand down is knowing your rights.

Every young man of color needs to know how to respond to authority. He needs to know when it is appropriate to express how he feels and when it is advantageous to remain silent.

I began writing this book in the midst of the Black Lives Matter (BLM) movement, founded in 2013 in response to Trayvon Martin's murder. The movement became a global organization with a mission to eradicate white supremacy and build local power to counter violence inflicted on Black communities [2]. Maybe the opinions of the BLM protesters was, if the individuals who occupy municipal offices and federal buildings refused to respond to phone calls, emails, and text messages, maybe they would pay attention to crowded streets, impassable intersections, and throngs of people blocking the doors to big box retailers.

The protesters had legitimate concerns that should be addressed. It could be argued that the problem was not the way the movement went about getting attention, but how others with issues critical to their own existence attached themselves, leaving room for the central agenda to be misconstrued. When you don't know how to appropriately express how you feel, especially regarding an issue that may not be shared by others, your opinion can be swallowed up in misunderstandings.

Rights can be defined as those moral or legal entitlements to have or obtain something, or to act in a certain way. For example, you have a right to vote and to express yourself, as long as you don't infringe on the rights of someone else. You have the right to learn and choose your own profession. Knowing your rights will direct how you respond to authority and react to life's situations.

Growing up in my mother's house, there were things that happened at her command I did not agree with, such as walking to the grocery store. I hated having to walk all the way there and back again, all within a certain time frame. The trip seemed like a thousand miles…one way.

I was always directed to make a list because if I forget something, I would have to go back and return in an even shorter amount of time. Many times, I did not make a list and one day it caught up with me. When I had to go back, I made the awful mistake of saying, "I don't think it was right that I had to make a second trip."

After I collected myself from the floor and made the second trip to the grocery store, I had to hear a "days-long" speech about what rights I had in my mother's house. With each iteration of the speech, my mother ended with, "This is my @#$%^ house and I say what goes!"

Years later, I agree; I lived in my mother's castle, she was the Queen. She set the rules and the only right I had was to obey them. My misunderstanding of how those rules worked encouraged me to react in a way that was not profitable to me. I complied with my mother's rules, even though I thought I had rights. When you feel like your rights are being infringed upon, understand your rights within that given situation. Demanding rights that are superseded by a ruling authority (whatever the situation) could make things worse in the long run.

Know Your Responsibilities

There is a difference between rights, responsibilities, and respect. Authority is power given to parents, teachers, elected officials, pastors, and even police. Each of these authority figures are given some level of responsibility to do a job. Let's revisit the story of the staffer I mentioned earlier.

The next morning, the staffer carelessly walked into my office to apologize for their behavior. I responded to the staffer that I was very disappointed in their actions and that such behavior was never to happen again. At this point, I was preparing for things to be better or worse, but I was not prepared for the confusion.

The staffer looked as though I said something foreign. They asked, "What do you mean." I calmly reminded them that for some time, I'd graced them with time and space to grow into their job. However, the line between "feel free to vent" and insubordination had been blurred when they chose to raise their voice.

I made it clear I had reached my limit with their performance issues, as well as leniency, and any lack of professionalism was no longer acceptable.

The staffer's posture went from jovial to defensive in a split-second. If humans had billboards on their foreheads, this one would have read, "I'm pissed and I've checked out." Funny thing; the same flashing sign was on my forehead.

In my professional opinion, and, as the authoritative figure in the scenario, whatever the staffer had to say in their defense was equivalent to an excuse. By then, my foot was tapping and my eyebrow was raised, my jaw was clenching and I clasped my hands continuously, trying not to make a fist. I was thinking to myself, "Are you seriously kidding me? You are about to be fired and you have the nerve to raise your voice?"

However, I quickly concluded that this intended correction was going nowhere and a back-and-forth verbal exchange would only lower me, as a leader, to a place I would regret. I had a choice to either pull rank, or maintain control of the moment.

Everything in me wanted to stand up…but wisdom kicked in, and I reminded the staffer of the primary issue. I calmly ended the conversation with a brief statement: "This will be noted. Just do your job."

The staffer left my office. For the rest of the day, the staffer had become a one-man beehive.

Everything that should have been going on was going on wonderfully. I think the staffer realized (whether they liked being reprimanded or not) they were out of order and had the potential to be fired. I knew my responsibility as a leader was to maintain my standard and integrity and leave it up to the staffer to rise to the occasion. In this situation, my decision to step up and set boundaries with the staffer, as well as the staffer's decision to step down and work with renewed optimism, led to a positive outcome

Responsibility is the duty to deal with something or, in some cases, it may involve having control over someone else's decision. Knowing what you are responsible for influences how you respond to authority. In the story of the staffer, you will see how he was aware of his responsibility to stand down and offer an apology, while I was aware of my responsibility to stand up and outline clear boundaries as the leader in the interaction. It is imperative you know your responsibility in every situation before you make the choice to stand up or stand down. This is a lesson I learned as a college freshman.

I attended and graduated from THE greatest institution of higher learning, an HBCU roughly forty minutes northwest of Houston, Texas: Prairie View A&M University!

Back then, registration was not a sophisticated as it is now. There was no "online" registration, no "online" housing reservations, and certainly no "online" financial aid. In fact, the one thing most people from that era would agree is that you were going to stand "in-line" for registration, "in-line" for housing reservations, and my favorite, "in-line" for financial aid.

During the first weeks on campus, you could stand in line for an entire day to go from one station to another. Sidebar: registration was usually when you made some of the most lifelong friendships. Those people would hold your place in line for day one, two, and day three! When you did make it to the front of any line, the last thing you wanted to hear was you needed another document. Everyone knew that meant you'd have to start all over again.

One day, after enduring several exhausting days of standing in line, I got to the cashier's window and the woman said those dreaded words: "You're missing something." She held up a blank page and said, "This is what you need" and told me to come back when I had the correct document.

In seconds, I was overtaken by a spirit of frustration. I commenced to telling her how I had just stood in line for what felt like forever and how it was her responsibility to make sure I knew this before allowing me to stand so long in line.

Little did I know, she was "Ms. B"- a legend at Prairie View A&M. Everyone loved Ms. B.

On this day, like a cross between an angry mother and a sixth-grade teacher, Ms. B. responded that as a young Black man who just graduated from high school and was admitted to the university, it was my responsibility to make sure I had all I needed when I left home.

With her index finger extended and pointing right

at me, she went on to say it was my responsibility to read the directions for registration before I left my room if I expected to complete the process. She was firing off at me so fast I felt like I was shrinking right where I stood. Sidebar: the room was filled with tons of students all around me. I felt like I was in one of those TV commercials where I was in the middle of a room and everyone was laughing at me. I knew in that moment I'd made a mistake I would never live down. Over thirty years later, I still get reminded of "that day when…"

Oddly enough, I do remember Ms. B. ending the scolding with "when you have THIS document, come back and ask for me." With my pride decimated, I left the office with a "Yes, Ma'am."

When I graduated, my mind flashed with the memory of Ms. B. asking me "Whose responsibility is it?"

While I was so busy reminding Ms. B. of her responsibilities, I failed to fulfill my own. Before you fill your chest with a need to "check" someone else on their responsibilities, make sure you've done your part.

Know How To Respect Yourself & Others

Respect is the final component to this chapter. It is one of the most vital because knowing the true meaning of respect influences how you respond to others. Sometimes it's better to say nothing, rather than say or do the wrong thing.

There is a saying that goes, "Chewing crow is a hard thing to do." Acting out and having to return and apologize can be a hard thing to do, but especially when the acting out was unwarranted or uncalled for. This was clear in the example of the staffer who had to go back and apologize and even more evident when I had to (respectfully) stand up to my superior later that day.

After the productive conversation with the staffer, my own resolve was tested. My superior called about a major blunder the organization made with several students. While the responsible department was not mine. I was the other stakeholder.

I knew this supervisor had a history of taking no ownership or accountability for mishaps. When I realized that his superior was on the other line, I expected this call would be no different. My superior proceeded to have me explain what happened. I was stunned because the blunder didn't happen in my department and I'd already shared with him what the responsible department had already done to correct this issue. Sidebar: being thrown under the bus is real.

In this case, I was in awe of how the situation played out. I took a deep breath to focus my response, but as I began to recount, my superior started interrupting me. Throughout my report, she kept interjecting with what she'd done.

By now, my foot was tapping, I was holding my forehead with my hand and waving my arms through the air in frustration. As the superior continued to interject, it was clear to me that she had been misinformed or at best, underinformed. I knew this was going to be a "pass the blame;" whether on me or on someone else, but in that moment, while angry enough to spit, I knew my position. I was the lowest on the ladder: because of who I was talking to and who was also listening in, I had the choice to "be right" or "come out looking like the bad guy."

However, I had to be clear that what needed to happen at my level was done by the book, including getting my superior's approval at every interval. I also needed to make sure that her superior knew that corrective measures had already been taken without throwing my superior under the bus.

In the end, I reminded my superior of her question and responded with a solid answer. I calmly reminded her superior of the process, according to policy, and recounted each step that was taken. I assured them that the issue had been taken care of and the students were satisfied. My superior simply ended the call with a "thank you" and everyone left satisfied.

Without embarrassing anyone, the ownership of error in this situation was eventually made clear. Regardless of whether or not I ever hear a "thank you," I trust that because my respect saved someone's dignity, the favor will be paid forward.

Respect is a feeling of deep admiration for someone elicited by their abilities, qualities, or achievements. For example, walking around two people while they are talking instead of walking between them is showing respect. Choosing not to make fun of someone's tattered shoes is an example of respect. Listening to someone tell their side of a story before sharing yours is an example of respect.

I remember surfing YouTube for a video to use in a class lecture when I came across a video clip of popular rapper. I stopped to view it, as I was not familiar with the rap star or his music. In the video, the rapper had come into the studio to do a live interview. Early in the interview, the host had apparently made fun of the rapper's name. The rapper was ranting and raving and using aggressively foul language when speaking to the host and it became obvious the host was using the rapper's name in a way that he did not appreciate.

In the video, the host had a smile on his face, but the rapper was clearly about to blow a gasket. During the short time together, the host kept implying that something was bothering the rapper and kept pressing the rapper to explain why he appeared to be so upset. Each time the host would ask what was the matter, the rapper would simply say "put some respect on my name." Each time the host would ask the same question, the rapper would respond the same way. However, the rapper's response would get louder and more intense. This went on for nearly two minutes. On live radio or television, that feels like a much longer time.

Suddenly, the rapper stood up and tossed his headphones on the soundboard. I just knew the two were headed for a battle. Instead, the rapper turned and headed for the door. As he was going out of the door, guess what he shouted?

You guessed it. He said, "PUT SOME RESPECT ON MY NAME!"

Later that day, Birdman (the rapper) called the

radio show host and apologized for carrying on the way he did while on the show. Incidentally, there was no other mention of that situation again. Although I am not sure who was at fault, both the host and the rapper were remembered for how they resolved their issue with each other.

It is imperative that Black men know how to respond to authority. That means you have to know your rights, responsibilities, and respect. You have to know when and how to execute each. There were several times in life where I executed the right plan in the wrong manner. Some things were better left unsaid and done. The next time you are in a situation where you feel like you are being disrespected, I challenge you to step back and breathe. If you are to stand your ground, the opportunity for you to do so will come again. It only takes one misstep and your credibility is destroyed.

In both situations, with my superior and the staffer, I felt like I would have been justified in standing up and protecting my own position. I would have been well within my rights to "fire back." Had I done so, in both cases, I would have been marked as hostile or aggressive. I would have been deemed the one not being a "team player" or a "supportive leader."

Personal Application

For the Black man struggling with knowing when to stand up…or stand down, I advise him to take a moment and remember that people bring their personal lives and personal deficiencies to the workplace, shared community space, and even home. You must know your role when interacting with people. Stand down until you are sure it is time to stand up and when you stand up, be sure to preserve your integrity and the dignity of those involved.

4

KNOW HOW TO COMMUNICATE CLEARLY

"When you open your mouth, know the occasion, the audience and your role..."
-Byron Dickens

The Importance of Clear Communication

Clear communication requires a willingness to be intentional and present in every interaction. When one speaks clearly, words are carefully chosen and appropriate for the occasion. My godfather taught me the importance of choosing my words carefully and communicating clearly.

I'll never forget a time when I needed money for books, food, and some "spending money" for an upcoming road trip with a college student organization I was a part of. I asked him if I could "borrow" some money. He asked how much I needed and what my plans were for spending the money. I mumbled an amount, thinking he would go through the roof. He didn't, so I gladly told my godfather exactly what I was going to do with the money, including the road trip. He said "Sure, Ok" and took the money out of his pocket. Elated, I told him "Thank you" and began to walk away. Suddenly, my godfather said, "Hey" and I knew by the tone in his voice there was something else to talk about. He asked, "When are you going to pay me back?" I thought to myself, "Pay you back?" and quickly shouted, "I really meant, "Can you give me some money?" He responded with a smirk on his face, replying, "You asked to borrow some money. When you borrow something, you pay it back."

I was frozen. He'd never asked me to pay anything back, but I remembered that I'd never asked to "borrow" anything from him either. I stumbled, "I don't know." Sidebar: my godfather was a very giving man, but a very conscientious spender. I was really praying that he was only joking. He wasn't.

He said to me, "I will give you one month to pay me back every penny you borrowed" and followed with, "A man says what he means and means what he says."

Needless to say, I not only paid my godfather back the full amount I'd borrowed, but I was also forever careful of every word I spoke to him, especially when I needed something from him.

Every young man of color needs to know how to

communicate effectively. The notion that whatever we say is acceptable leaves us open to being perceived as incompetent or limited. I learned to choose my words carefully because they really do have power and meaning. I learned that it is important to make sure the words I use are conveying the message I intend for others to receive.

Every culture or group has its own way of communicating within itself; you have alternative capital, or "another" way of communicating. I used to teach my students that they were bilingual; they spoke both standard English and Ebonics (a dialect or form of communication used by 80% to 90% of African Americans at some time or another) [3]; that's cultural collateral. You have what is necessary to operate impactfully in two cultures. The challenge is to learn to be able to fluently speak both. I remember the movie, BlacKKKlansman: When rookie officer "Stallworth" (John David Washington) was asked how he could speak so clearly and effectively and then change his accent. He responded, "I speak the King's

English and Jive!"

Many times, our cultures give us "a pass," but that pass is only good inside that specific culture. The problem is that many of us never learn what is correct and appropriate outside of our culture. Too often, thinking one way of communicating fits all situations means we live in the delusion that "they know what I mean." It is important to know how and when to adjust because everyone does not know what you mean.

When you can communicate clearly and effectively in a variety of situations, everyone knows it. Conversely, when your communication skills are limited to only a few settings, everyone knows this as well. It is important to understand how what you say, when you say it, and the tone you say it with helps you communicate more effectively. Knowing the occasion, the audience, and your role will assist you in being a clear communicator and carefully choosing appropriate words to use.

Know The Occasion

There is not always a set time to interact with someone. A conversation can break out at any time. However, there is always a reason or occasion why a conversation is happening. Knowing the occasion for why you are speaking helps you communicate more effectively.

Conversations can be formal or informal or they can suddenly change from formal to informal, and vice versa. Conversations can be serious but suddenly transition when someone starts laughing because the conversation becomes amusing. It is important to keep the occasion in the front of your mind when engaging in conversation, no matter the direction it may go. Move with the conversation in the appropriate direction based on the occasion. Occasion lays the foundation for the length and depth of the conversation. Knowing the reason for speaking can, and will, save embarrassment, arguments, and blunders.

There will be many times when you will be called

on to say something or write something and when this happens, it is utterly important to be clear of the occasion. When you can communicate effectively based on the occasion, it shows.

I have attended many funerals and memorials. At each of them, there was an allotted time for friends and loved ones to share lasting memories of the deceased. At these events, it was pretty clear why people had gathered and anyone that stood to speak should address their comments to the family of and about the deceased.

I remember attending one funeral and of course, the directions on the obituary said "Two-minutes, please." A young man rose, approached the podium, and began to speak. He started by telling everyone how long he knew the "guest of honor." Then suddenly, the comments shifted to how he himself had done some bad things in life but how his family was his everything. He went on to say how happy he was when his son was born, that he was a straight "A" student and was now attending college. I assumed he was going to find a way to tie his comments into his relationship with the deceased, but he never did, he just went on and on about his son.

At this point, the family of the deceased was no longer smiling, the officiant was sitting on the edge of his seat, and I heard someone should out "Amen!" In the Black church, "Amen" meant one of two things: either someone agreed with you, or someone was hinting for you to sit down.

He didn't get the message, even when the background music stopped. It wasn't until the officiant stood and asked him to be seated that it finally registered. I thought to myself, "Who does that?"

Initially, I was embarrassed for the young man, but then I was angry because he made this occasion about himself and his family.

It is easy to get carried away with self-centered conversations when the occasion for conversing is not at the forefront of your mind. I am sure the speaker may have intended to say some kind things about the deceased, but he missed the mark that day. If we are honest, it has happened to us all at some point or another. When communicating, it is also necessary to read the audience. When you are clear on who you are speaking or writing to, their way of receiving information, it is easier to focus on the occasion and keep the listener engaged. When communicating it is also necessary to read the audience. Doing this will keep you focused on the occasion and engaged with your listener.

Know Your Audience

An audience is one or more people that are positioned to listen to another speak or convey a message. Audiences may or may not share backgrounds, experiences, or expertise. Knowing the audience you are conversing with helps you communicate more effectively. For example, audiences may be a best friend, a sibling, or a boss or government official.

I remember attending an awards ceremony on

campus where students presented awards to distinguished individuals around campus. As each of the students approached the podium to speak, they all used the same phrases. One of the phrases that stuck in my head was "You know what I'm saying." They repeated it so much I was embarrassed for them. In my head, I was thinking, "Why didn't someone practice with them?" Remember, cultures have their own rules for communicating. Also, there are different types of audience. While "you know what I'm saying" might be acceptable among friends in a casual setting, this was a formal occasion and the audience was professional. Casual language was not appropriate.

I thought back to the time I wrote my first speech in college. I thought the speech was pretty good. I had all the part in the right places for a speech. The introduction, the body, and conclusion were all perfectly balanced. I had a solid thesis statement, and supporting details. I presented the speech with some level of confidence.

However, instead of getting an "A" on the assignment, there was a note attached saying, "See me after class." When I met with the professor, she explained that the content of my speech was proper and concise but I was not using scholarly language. She said that my speech sounded like I was talking to my friends at the dorm. Sidebar: be careful of thinking too much of yourself. There is a thin line between confidence and arrogance. When you cross the line, you can get chewed up and spat out. While I was extremely embarrassed, the professor made sure I didn't take her corrections as an attack. She went on to say that my audience was a university speech class and not the quad. I never forgot that moment.

Fast-forward to the campus awards ceremony. For the students I was watching, I wanted to rush to the stage and say "See me after class." Even though they had friends sitting in the audience, the occasion was formal, thus it was important to speak to a formal audience. Like my own experience, all I could thing about was that their communication skills were limited to a particular audience and in that moment, everyone knew it.

Know Your Role

The person leading a conversation hopes to accomplish a purpose with their communication, so they take on the leadership role in the conversation. Knowing your role in a conversation helps you communicate more effectively. In most cases, the role is to inform or to persuade. When informing, the intent is to explain something, give more information, or tell how to do something. When persuading, the intent is to have the listener change how they feel or think about a particular issue.

In the last chapter, I shared how I was engaged in a tense conversation with a staffer of mine, followed by another exchange with my boss. In both situations my role in the conversations was unclear, but shortly in, I needed to define my role.

Initially, my role in the conversation with my staffer was to encourage them to pay closer attention to the quality of their work. Knowing my audience, I knew a direct approach would probably make the room stale, but I also needed to make my expectations clear. The response I received was somewhat expected, so my role in the conversation shifted to persuasion. In this instance, I took the lead and chose to speak more than listen.

In the interaction with my boss, my role was to inform. After several minutes of questioning, it was clear that the only thing needed from me was information. If I would have failed to remember my role in the conversation, the focus would have shifted, unnecessarily, to me.

When you know your role in a conversation or exchange with someone, it is easier to maintain clear and effective communication. Whether it is noted or not, people understand the need to maintain roles in a conversation.

There will be times when you want to "go off" on someone who approached you in a way that was inappropriate to you. You may be the authority figure in a given situation or the subject of someone else's authority. Either way, understanding your occasion and audience will make the difference between a hostile environment and a climate of respect.

Personal Application

When you are called into an exchange with someone, and signals are flying everywhere, pause for a moment to breathe. I challenge you to breathe, even if that means taking deep breaths every other sentence. Remind yourself of the sole purpose of the conversation. Be mindful of who you are engaging with, then, decide what your role is in the conversation. Clear communication is attainable to anyone who masters knowing the occasion, audience, and their role in the discussion.

5

KNOW HOW TO RESOLVE A CONFLICT

"Whenever you're in conflict with someone, there is one fact that can make the difference between damaging your relationship and deepening it. That factor is attitude."
~William James

The Importance of Conflict Resolution

When was the last time you had an altercation with someone that should not have happened? Did you regret it? Well I have and yes, I regretted it.

I have never been one for confrontation or arguments but there's a first time for everything. The first time I lived away from home was when I went away to college. Granted, Prairie View was not what some would consider "away from home," but to me, if I was more than 10 miles from my village. I was away from home.

In the freshman dorm, most guys lived with two other roommates. If you arrived on campus and checked in first, you got best pick of bed and locker. Growing up with two uncles and three male cousins, living with guys was no big deal. However, living with strangers was something different altogether.

Back in my village, no matter how many of us there were in a house, the rules were the same- make your bed, don't lay around in your "good clothes" and take a bath every night. It was the same rule at my mother's house, my aunt's house, and my grandparents' house. I thought it was the same at everyone's house. Boy, was I wrong.

In college, I learned that not everyone did their laundry on a regular basis. I learned that not everyone wiped the water off the bathroom floor after showering. I found out that not everyone took the same approach to personal hygiene. Sidebar: growing up in Texas, summers were very hot. We didn't have all the video games to keep us pinned to the computer screen. Children entertained themselves outside. You'd always hear my grandmother saying to one of us, "You better get outside! Close my door! Stop letting out my "good air." In fact, that was common among most of the grandmothers on our street. After we'd been running and playing in the hot Texas sun, we would acquire a certain "aroma." Trust me, it wasn't a pleasant aroma.

I remember my grandmother saying to me, "I hear you" after we'd been playing outside all afternoon. At first, I never understood what she meant. Being the smarty pants I was, I'd respond with "But, Big Mama, I didn't say anything." She'd then give me a certain look. In my family, a look could have a thousand meanings. However, I knew this look was one that suggested I should vacate the room immediately. I learned that it was her way of saying I was musty and needed to take care of it immediately. She always did it without embarrassing me.

One of my college roommates would consistently come in from the gym with an "aroma;" one I easily recognized from my childhood. He'd take off his workout gear, throw the items in the closet, jump right in bed, and off to sleep he would go. My other roommate and I were amazed by this ritual. After a few minutes, you guessed it; the whole room would be singing with his "aroma."

After a few days, his bed would be dingy and smelly. No matter how much we kept the windows opened, the room always smelled. Many years ago, recording artist, Lionel Richie sang, "There comes a time when you hear a certain call..." Well, there came a time and I heard a certain call. Remember when I talked about knowing when to stand up…and when to stand down? This was a time to stand up.

I had enough of living in the smelly room. If you remember the air freshener television commercial that said the person had become "odor blind? That to others the space had become a large stinky sock, or a doggy car?" That was our dormitory. It was time to say something to my roommate about the odor issue. It would have been easy to get crazy if this roommate was a horrible person, but he was a good man and I wanted things to go well.

As I contemplated approaching him, I thought about how bad this could go. I could hear my grandmother saying "Just say I hear you." I could say that, but I understood that while I needed to say something, I didn't need to embarrass him. I needed to show him grace. Remember, you have to know who you're talking to, why you're talking to them, and what your role is in the conversation. Words have power and I didn't want this to come between us.

That evening when my roommate came in, he completed his usual ritual: took his gym gear off, tossed it in closet, and jumped in bed. I called his name and asked if I could talk to him about something. He looked as though he knew something was not right. I shared with him about the odor coming from his closet and his bed. Without a word, he jumped up, got dressed, and stormed out of the room. The other roommate looked at me speechless. For the rest of the night, I felt horrible. Maybe I'd offended him in some way. Then I thought, "Wait, that odor offends me!"

The next day, my roommate came back into the room and asked if he could talk to me. I thought, "Oh dang! It's about to get ugly in here." I was wrong.

First, he dropped his head and apologized about the odor. Then, with rounded shoulders, he apologized for making us uncomfortable. Then he said when got some money he would wash his clothes and bedcoverings. He had this look of defeat on his face, as if he had been fighting something or someone and could no longer continue. I knew the reason why he'd allowed things to go so far was because he couldn't afford the essentials that I took for granted. In that moment, I was speechless. If I could have crawled under the nearest bed, I would have. I realized that not only had I embarrassed him, but I knew how he was feeling firsthand.

Back then, many of us came to college with very little money. Most of our parents would send monthly allowances. Regardless of how you used the money you had, when it was gone, it was gone. Sidebar-my grandparents were the business owners, not my parents. I want to be clear; my parents were "barely making it themselves." While there were two adult parents in my house, most of the time, there was only one source of income. The seasonal work of a construction worker only made room for the essentials. There was no room for waste. Every penny counted. I knew exactly what he was going through in that moment. I immediately assured him that I understood. For the rest of that year, I made sure my care packages from home included enough for the two roommates, and yes, there was always enough bath soap and detergent to go around.

The situation could have gone wrong on so many levels. The one thing a Black man will defend with his life is his pride. My roommate could have (attempted) to "whoop my @#$%^!" He could have decided not to come back to the room, ever. He could have done all sorts of things in response to me bringing attention to his situation. To be a respectful Black man in the Black man culture, you always leave another Black man with his dignity!

My roommate calmly shared his situation with me. I could clearly understand every word. Fortunately, because he owned his part in the conflict, it forced me to listen and own my part.

Every man of color needs to know how to resolve conflict. He needs to know how to agree to disagree and walk away. Conflict resolution among African American males shapes and influences interpersonal communications, beliefs about causes of problems, and problem-solving approaches[5]. The media and "alternative truths" would have one think that shouting and over-talking, fighting, and retaliating against someone who has offended you is the best way to handle an altercation. The problem today is when two young men disagree, the end result is usually not good. A cycle of retaliation, hurt, and harm typically starts. When you know how to resolve conflict you help reduce miscommunication and create opportunities for appreciation of others and their perspectives.

However, when you don't have the tools to reach a peaceful resolution, the world sees you not as the intelligent leader you are, but only as an individual not civil enough to work things out with others. Listening, being civil, and remaining open are tools for resolving conflict. In order to resolve conflict, you have to master active listening, empathy, and impartiality.

Active Listening

Active listening is a tool for resolving conflict. It is

more than just waiting for an opportunity to put your two cents in. It is a form of communication that requires you to concentrate, understand the other person's perspective, and remember the content of the conversation.

For example, when there is an altercation between two people you know, you can show you are actively listening by restating what one of your friends said before the other starts to speak. In other words, show them you are listening actively by repeating what they say.

Asking your friends probing questions also shows you are actively listening to them. You show you are actively listening by affirming how both of your friends feel at the moment. That not only shows you are listening, but also that you understand where they are (emotionally) at the time.

When my roommate came back into the room, he did not storm back in. He did not come in shouting and screaming. I was prepared to fight or at least, say whatever else was on my mind. However, his posture and approach were non-confrontational. He began by asking me if he could speak to me. In that moment, the ball was in my court. If we were going to resolve our issue, it would have to start with me listening. As he spoke, his shoulders drooped and his voice lowered. While he talked, it took everything in me not to interrupt. I quickly realized that he needed to not only apologize, but also vent about the challenges in his life. By just listening, I learned that like many of us, he was the first to go off to college. But unlike myself, he didn't have the support of a village to send him off. There was no money for a bus ticket home every weekend. There was no one to send him a coat for the winter months on "the Hill." By listening, I understood why he wouldn't spend money on soap. He not only had little money, but very little of anything else.

In his gentle approach and my listening, there was an opportunity for healing between two young, Black men with the hopes of becoming "somebody" before they left the academy. He was able to purge some things, as many of us do. I was able to appreciate the fact that while life wasn't all I thought it should have been, here was a living being, standing in my face, who had far less than I did.

Your ability to concentrate on someone's perspective or "where they are coming from" during a disagreement is a tool that helps you resolve conflict. Often, conflicts can be avoided by taking the time to listen for understanding. Instead of attempting to argue your point, listen, and find common ground to help neutralize an escalating situation.

Empathy

Empathy is a civil tool for resolving conflict. It is genuinely understanding how someone else is feeling. We show empathy when conflict arises as a result of loss or damage. We show empathy when conflict arises as a result of someone being offended by someone else. Empathy is the way we show we have put ourselves in someone else's situation. Statements like, "I know how you're feeling," "I don't understand how they could do such a thing," or "I can't believe that just happened to you," show that you are sincerely feeling the same emotions your friend is feeling.

When my roommate was apologizing for making me and our other roommate uncomfortable, it was important to do more than just accept his apology. I needed to do more than just sit there and listen. After all, this was another Black man putting his dignity on the line to resolve conflict. Sidebar-all a Black man has is his dignity. He will defend it at all costs, even against his own family. When he puts either of them on the line, it is urgent to know how serious the matter has become. It was just as important that I showed I understood why he was apologizing and what he was apologizing for (we will discuss knowing your why in the next chapter). Showing empathy meant I needed to genuinely nod my head in agreement, showing him I was present in the moment. I needed to say, "Hey man, I get it."

Unfortunately, Black men have been institutionalized into mistrusting one another.

Sidebar-Read the Willie Lynch Letter. It goes into extensive detail about how slavery and institutional racism intentionally pitted us (Black men) against each other. The impact is still present today but empathy can fix this.

When I showed I really understood where my roommate was coming from (empathy), he shared more about himself, and we found we really had a lot in common. In that moment, I had a choice to either put myself in his situation, creating a safe space for one Black man to trust another, or leave him there, without a simple opportunity to trust me.

Your ability to understand how someone feels during a disagreement is a tool that helps you resolve conflict. People often make decisions and use words that stem from unresolved past pain and disappointment which has nothing to do with you. Give people an opportunity to share how they feel, and respect that time with your attention and regard. The conversation will take a positive turn if you show you care.

Impartiality

As I was attempting to resolve a conflict with roommate #1, I noticed that roommate #2 did not engage. At least, it appeared that he was not getting involved. Before the conversation, roommate #2 was in agreeance with everything I had issues with. However, when I expressed my concerns with roommate #1 and he with me, roommate #2 had nothing to contribute. Initially, I thought it wasn't right, but then I considered, maybe I'd just opened the can of worms and I had to handle it by myself. Sidebar: never take on a situation or conversation with others you are not willing to, or cannot handle on your own.

I quickly came to understand that roommate #2 was practicing impartiality. So that neither of us would feel like he was taking sides, or that we were being outnumbered, roommate #2 remained neutral. There were times in the conversation when we talked over one another and many times, our voices were raised. We even got in each other faces. Like many

Black men, we were very passionate about our points-of-view.

Remember, the one thing a Black man protects is his dignity. Each time we would raise our voices, or a comment seemed perplexing, roommate #2 would repeat what was said for clarity. He would say, "So what you're saying is…" This not only presented an opportunity for both of us to be heard, but also ensured the intended message was not misunderstood. Sidebar: there is a difference between what one person says and what the listener actually hears (perception). Impartiality allows the conversation to be clear for all involved.

In the struggle of being a Black man in America, where we are constantly defending our integrity against forces outside of the village, it is a matter of life and death that we know how to resolve conflict, especially among ourselves. This means you have to master active listening, empathy, and impartiality.

There have been a few scenarios where I did not resolve issues in a productive way. Yes, I've allowed meaningless things to come between me and another Black man. As a result, lifelong wedges arose between myself and others. However, since learning the skill of conflict resolution, I've been able to go back and mend a few of those relationships. Conflict resolution can be used within families, friend circles, your community, and the workplace.

Personal Application

The next time you are at odds with someone, don't allow simple misunderstandings to cancel what could be a great relationship. Practice listening to hear exactly what the person is saying. Make understanding where the other person is coming from the ultimate goal. When you are not the one in conflict, make sure you are not taking sides, especially before you have all the facts. Choose relationships over being right because without having to prove your point: what is right always finds its way to the light.

6

KNOW HOW TO PLAN
FOR SUCCESS

---

*"Sometimes, you need to feel the pain and
sting of defeat to activate the real passion and
purpose that God predestined for you."*
~Chadwick Boseman

Success Can Be Planned

Think of a time when you know you needed to do something but just didn't know how? Did it involve just you or did it include others? If so, you're not alone. We have all been there. Each semester, I have my students make a one-on-on appointment with me; an opportunity to find out how to best serve them without the social pressure of being in the large class setting.

During this time, I always ask them the same leading questions of "What's your major?" "Why did you select this major?" and "How can I be an asset to you, not just in this course, but in your collegiate career?" I would share with them some stages that they should plan for as the matriculate at the university. As a freshman, I tell them that they should plan to want to do everything they thought they were "grown" enough to do-from staying up to see if the streetlights will go off, to going to every party on campus. As a sophomore, I tell students to plan on learning their own tolerance levels and limits-from who you can and cannot get along with, to balancing a social calendar and their GPA. I tell students that during their junior year, they should plan on getting great internships and focusing on professional courses. Finally, as seniors, they should plan on building professional networks, graduation, and landing their first job. Sidebar- nothing makes sitting in commencement sweeter that knowing you already have a job!

In Black families, there will be a huge party after the graduation ceremonies. Family and friends will come from far and wide to celebrate your/their accomplishments.

However, after the party is over and the decorations have been taken down, parents will want to have that discussion about your plan for where you will go to live and work on Monday! I go through this exercise with students to lay the foundation for discussions on planning their collegiate success.

Like my early college days, most students do not give much thought to planning for their own success beyond graduation; I know I was just glad to be on campus.

As a first-gen, I was going to college. Beyond that, I thought everything else would just fall in place. Like me, many students are still existing under the plans their families have imposed on them. Because there was no one with college experience, families were and are proud to say "My child is going to college!" Like many families such as mine, parents expect if they get their students to the gate, the university will do the rest. Boy are they wrong, just like in my time.

As I alluded to earlier, when I got to college, there was registration for this and that. Sign up for this class or that class, go to this building for this and to another building for that. I felt so "dumb" for not knowing so many things. But, I was willing to do it because my parents planned for me to attend college, graduate, and get a good job. Had it not been for the likes of Mr. Bill Chapman, sponsor of the Baptist Student Movement and Mrs. March Tramble, my freshman advisor, I would not have successfully navigated my college experience.

I cannot count how many times I've spoken to students on the brink of graduation who do not have a plan for the rest of the month, let alone the rest of their lives. They spent four, five, and sometimes six years taking courses at a university but failed to plan for life after the university. As an educator, I dove intentionally into deep conversations with students to show them one truth: from the time they come though the pale brick university gates, they were in a safe space and were encouraged to discover and cultivate the person that's been quietly living and growing in their head and heart. I would share with them, in order to navigate their own lives after graduation, they would have to start planning for their success now.

Do you know your Purpose?

Every Black man needs to know his life's purpose. He needs to know how to plan for success. To demonstrate the importance of this concept, consider the following:

In a YouTube video, comedian Michael Jr. asks a Black male, music director to sing "Amazing Grace." The man sings the song in a very operatic voice and the crowd applauds.

Then Michael asks him to sing the song like his uncle had just been released from prison or as if he'd just been shot in the back and survived. The man belts out a long, Southern, Black Baptist version of the same song. The audience erupts with cheers and ovations!

Michael points out that the first time the man sang "Amazing Grace" (with passion), it demonstrated that he knew what he was singing.

The second version of the same song demonstrated that the man knew why he was singing. There is a difference.

The problem today is, many people focus on what to do to be successful, like going to college to get a degree to get a job. However, they don't focus on why being successful matters. For those that do get jobs in the professional area they studied, many leave after only a short time because there was no real reason for choosing that path. In order to plan for your success, you have to know your why.

Maybe for those who are unsatisfied within their field, it is because the why was not purposeful. Perhaps it was to survive something, to gain status, or even freedom. When your why is purposeful, you find fulfillment even if the salary is not substantial. There are no titles, and accolades are not attached.

Purpose makes you happy. It brings you unexplainable joy and it serves other people. When your why is survival, status, or freedom, you often spend valuable time trying to fulfill a plan designed for you by others, unexpected life situations, or uncontrollable circumstances.

Do you Know what Motivates you?

There are three steps to planning for your success. The first step in planning for your success is identifying your motivation. Motivation is an internal or external drive to accomplish a certain goal. Motivation is your why which drives your plan for success.

For example, helping to improve your neighborhood's condition is a form of motivation. Wanting to know what it feels like to live in another country is another. Perhaps wanting financial independence within a year is another motivator.

When I decided to go to college, my motivation was freedom! All I wanted to do was get out of my parent's house. I didn't want to follow any more of their rules. I wanted to make my own plans and do my own thing. College was just the ticket. I would be able to come and go as I pleased. After all, I was grown. In my head, the only person I needed was me. Boy, was I wrong, because that motivation would soon fade away.

Eventually, my motivation for going to college shifted into something else: status. There was an inner payoff to hearing people laud my accomplishments when I returned home for visits. I noticed, people treated you differently when they realized that you were a college student. I remember working part-time at a department store and each evening, rushing in from campus all the older Black ladies would say, "There's Professor" and I loved it.

After graduation, I got my first job. Everywhere I went, people who knew me would refer to me as "the teacher." After all, I was the first to graduate with a college degree in my family. I had a really nice paycheck for a 24-year-old. After three "hoopties," I even bought a brand-new car, right off the showroom floor.

At some point though, the nicknames Professor and Teacher lost their glamour. I no longer cared about the status of being a college graduate.

It wasn't until my third year as a teacher when I found my purpose. I realized I actually made a difference in the lives of children who looked just like me. It was then that my motivation for success became solely to serve a purpose. My goal was to change as many lives as I could through education and

I needed do it intentionally. From that point on, I was like the energizer bunny.

Since my legacy was to reach out to the less fortunate (now that I had an income), I set goals to buy backpacks and supplies for every student in my class who didn't have them (more on that later).

I even asked my godmother (a baker) to make cookies for my students each week. She individually wrapped them, signing "From Granny," so they could all brag about what their "grandmother" did for them.

Sidebar- when you grow up in poverty, you might have grandparents but you might not be able to brag about them. When I could not buy things that my students needed, I solicited help from all of my college friends.

My largest project before leaving the classroom as a teacher was "Secret Santa." I had all of my student list 3 things they'd like for Christmas: 1. Something they needed for class, 2 and 3. Things they would love to have at home.

Sidebar: when you want to do something for one

student who lives in poverty and they have sibling, you have to do something for them as well. No parent wants one child getting nice gifts while other is left out

I solicited 25 of my college friends, mostly in other professions, told them what I was doing, and amazingly, everyone was on board to help.

I shared with my friends that some students had siblings and I'd need extra gifts for them. I was blown away with the fact that not only did these people agree to do more, they got their friends and coworkers in on the giving as well. I answered calls asking, "Can I get my "Secret Angel this?" "And that?" I remember spending a great deal of time telling Secret Santa's to stop buying.

On the day of the Christmas party, I decorated the school library. Of course, many were asking what was I doing, as most parties were in classrooms and at the end of the day. I'd shared my plan with my principal, who gladly gave me permission to use the larger space.

Just after the gifts and party favors had been

delivered and put in place, the principal came in. He looked around, took a seat and started crying! I asked he was alright and he simply reminded me of all the ways that I'd helped students in my class and the school, but this…this took the cake! He was amazed at the presents everywhere!

I invited parents to come to the party, especially to help students get their presents home safely. When they walked in, many parents burst into tears.

As I reflect on that day, my heart fills with joy and my eyes tear with remembrance. I knew firsthand what it felt like to not get new things on Christmas morning and for birthdays. Moreover, I knew what it must have been like for my parents to not be able to do more for their children; I understood the tears.

I explained to the parents that our class had Secret Santa's who wanted to remain anonymous. I shared that they had all purchased three gifts from a wish list that our students had prepared. I also shared with parents that the Secret Santa's wanted parents to sign their names on at least one of the gifts. The parents gladly signed their names and the class walked in. You can imagine the faces of those fourth graders, but can you imagine the faces of their parents?

My motivation had gone from freedom to purpose. Everyone has a purpose. Sometimes it takes a minute to realize your own purpose. In some cases, your purpose is to find your purpose. When you find it, you will work for free! That inner "someone" within me, whose drive was once status, changed into a desire to serve others. Once I tasted the success of servitude, I knew helping people become their best was now my why.

The next step in planning your success is identifying actions you need to take. Actions are those conscious or intentional things you do to accomplish a goal. Actions are what you do in your plan for success.

For example, volunteering is an action to improve your neighborhood's condition. When your goal is to experience living in another country, an action might be to search the internet for as much information on that country as possible. Talking to a financial planner is an action you can take when your goal is to become financially independent.

In previous chapters, I mentioned saying what you mean and meaning what you say. I'll add to that by including, doing what you say you're going to do. I was motivated by my purpose. My purpose was to help my students become the best they could be and to do this, I needed to set a goal. I needed a goal that was S.M.A.R.T.

Do You Know How to Create a S.M.A.R.T Goal?

A smart goal is specific; you have to be able to measure it. My goal had to be achievable and relative. It had to be timely. Here's what I mean: I needed to be very clear about what I wanted to do and I wanted to give away backpack and supplies. I needed to be clear on how many I wanted to give away; all 25 students in my class: and, in to order to make sure the goal was achieved, I set a timeline; before the second week of class. When there are no timelines and deadlines, things remain dreams and ideas, not guided projects.

In order to make sure I did what I said I was going to do and to make the goal become more than a dream or an idea, I needed to take action.

First, I shopped around to find backpacks and supplies for my students, which meant going from one store to another. Many times, I would have to return to a store to negotiate prices. Then, after I negotiated a price I could afford, I still needed help retrieving the supplies from the store. I solicited help from friends and family to deliver the supplies to my school, working around many different schedules (a difficulty for an impatient man like me).

Here was another instance when I needed to know when to stand up for my students and when to stand down and ask for help. Once all the supplies were collected, I placed the backpacks on the backs of each student's desk before they arrived. I was able to take many of the actions on my own. However, I needed help with others. I had family members price shop for me and friends picked up and delivered supplies to me. I needed the custodian to open the building early so I could stuff backpacks and assemble them on the desks.

However, when the students arrived, there was laughter and excitement for the first 30 minutes of class and it made every moment of effort worthwhile and purposeful.

A goal is just an idea or a dream, until you make it happen. Make your plan smart and doable, even if it means getting help. Be clear of what you need to do in order to achieve your goal. The most important thing is to do is something!

The final step in planning your success is activating your resilience. Resiliency is the ability to bounce-back when situations distract you from taking action. Resiliency is the how you keep going in your plan for success.

For example, when you desire to improve your community's condition by cleaning up the block, yet someone continues to throw trash on the ground, resiliency enables you to continue cleaning up the block until your example inspires others.

Resiliency enables you to keep searching when you cannot find information on a country you researched before. Resiliency is what you need to start saving money when an unexpected life situation happens and it demolishes your savings.

I was clear about my goal to help my students. I had a SMART plan. However, even the best plans can go wrong.

The week just before the big party, I received calls from Secret Santa's saying they could not shop for gifts. The good thing was they were not backing out, but the gifts were not purchased and there were only a few days left before the party. First, I was angry. How could someone agree to such a good thing and not follow through?

Well the reality was, this was my goal. It would be my responsibility to see it through. While they'd agreed to sponsor a student, the reality was, these people also had busy lives. To ensure no student was disappointed, I asked others to go out into the Christmas crowds again to shop. In some cases, I did the shopping myself. I stood in long lines, over several days, even gaining another Secret Santa while standing in line.

The morning of the party, the custodian was nowhere to be found. First, I was upset. Why did the janitor pick this morning to "goof off?" Then I was panicked. What was I going to do if the principal called the whole thing off or the presents started to arrive and they had to sit out in the hallway with no one to keep an eye on them? But, I was determined. To ensure the goal was achieved, I scoured the building to find someone with a key to that room who could stop what they were doing to help me. At the end of the day, thanks to resiliency, the party was a success.

It's one thing to have a goal. A goal could improve lives, be well-planned, have a good structure. Still, something could go wrong. As the old cliché goes, it doesn't matter how many times you get knocked down, it matters that you get up each time. The thing that kept me going was resilience and a determined mind to achieve the goal of not only making my students happy, but also making the parents a part of the process. I was determined that if I could not get things to go exactly the way I'd planned; the plan would still happen.

When you are in search of success, be clear of your why. Make sure you understand the motivations for your success. Commit to taking the necessary action to plan for your success.

I challenge you to find your purpose, then write a SMART plan for your success. Remember, that plan might be to find your purpose. Ask yourself, "What is my purpose?" If you already know, ask, "What do I need to do to achieve it?"

Be clear about what you are going to do and write it, type it, text it to yourself. Ask yourself, "Can this realistically be done?" The goal has to be achievable.

Personal Application

Since purpose is about serving people, make sure whatever you are going to do is about helping people. Write a date you intend to achieve the goal. Make a list of what you need to do to make things happen. Be clear on what things you can do on your own and what things you will need help with. Finally, put your plan on your mirror in the bathroom. Fold it, and put it in your wallet. Take it out every day and read it. Most importantly, don't quit!

7

KNOW HOW TO PRESENT YOURSELF

"You never get a second chance to make a first impression."-
-Will Rogers

The Power Of A First Impression

I once came across a plaque that read, "You never have a second chance to create a good first impression." The quote immediately led me to think about how it applies to what people wear, how people speak, and how they communicate with their body language in different environments. While many people have no problem creating a dynamic first impression, so many others get it wrong. The image people have of you is often how they classify you in their minds. Once you have said the wrong thing, your first words will never be forgotten. Once you show up wearing too much cologne, it will be the only thing you are remembered for. The way you present yourself on social media might not be the best for being remembered. However, when you control first impressions, people will never forget you...for the right reasons.

I was reading a few social media posts on the first African American president of the United States, Barack H. Obama. The posts went from his "pimp-walking" to the podium for press conferences, to "brushing his collar off "with Beyoncé," to "dropping the mike" after his last White House Correspondents' Dinner. There were posts about his singing Al Green's "Let's Stay Together" at the Apollo Theatre, "Sweet Home Chicago" with B.B. King, and "Amazing Grace" at the national memorial for nine African Americans killed by a White teenager during a prayer meeting at a church in Charlotte, South Carolina. All the posts concluded that the President of the United States had "swag."

This term promoted the idea that President Obama's entire presentation of himself exuded confidence. Self-confidence is the way a man demonstrates pride in himself. He is so self-assured that he is comfortable in his own skin, regardless of any opposition. President Obama's self-confidence was so noticeable that a popular daytime talk show host referred to a statement that his wife and First Lady, Michelle Obama, made: she said her husband's walk was "swagalicious." President Obama's confidence was apparent because he had mastered dressing and grooming himself appropriately, speaking confidently to any audience, and using his body language to communicate a message, without misrepresenting himself or losing his own identity in challenging situations.

Every young man of color needs to know how to present his best self, the first time. Fads, trends, and misinformation are traps that might give certain individuals a pass to be inappropriate in certain situations, usually resulting in misunderstandings and missed opportunities. The challenge today is that many guys think that to dress or speak a certain way is giving up their own identity or self-expression. I understand, but that is not the intent.

When you speak and dress to fit a certain situation, it is perceived you are "on your game" and you know how to appropriately fit into a given situation. Brand coach Bryan Dickens says, "People receive you based on how they perceive you. 55% of what people initially perceive of you is based on your appearance and body language. 38% of that perception is derived from your tone, pitch, and pace. Only 7% of other's initial perception of you is based on what you actually say. You are a walking logo of your personal brand!"

When you don't present yourself appropriately, it is often concluded that if you don't know when to wear a pair of Brogues instead of a pair of Jordan's, there may be other, more crucial things you don't know. While people might forget something good you did, they will never forget your first impression. Your attire and grooming, your conversation, and your posture help you present your best self the first time.

Attire

Choosing the appropriate attire and proper grooming helps you present your best self the first time. Attire is the way you use clothes or an outfit to present yourself appropriately to others for different occasions or situations.

There are three basic types of attire; casual, business, and formal. Of course there are fusions between each, but every occasion, situation, and setting has an appropriate attire. For example, jeans and sneakers are considered casual attire and are appropriate for Sunday Funday, going to class, or just hanging out with friends and family. However, when you are engaging in professional networking, or going to job interviews, business attire is more appropriate. An example of professional business attire would be a navy blue or charcoal grey suit, solid-colored shirt, a modest tie, and dark dress shoes. Sidebar: when you are going to an interview, research the company's website that you intend to work for.

Most websites will have company pictures. Some companies work in what's called "business casual;" usually less formal business attire, minus the tie and maybe dark jeans. If the team or staff members are wearing suits and ties in the pictures, you wear a suit and tie to the interview. It is easier to take off what you don't need. If nothing else, make sure you have on a professionally laundered shirt (pressed by the cleaners) and a tie.

On occasion, you will be invited to events that are considered formal, like a wedding, a dinner, or a gala, where formal, or "after five" attire, are appropriate. In these scenarios, you should wear a tuxedo, a satin tie, and patent leather shoes. In some cases, the attire might be "semi-formal" or "Sunday Best." That means a solid colored suit and tie. Most invitations, whether written or verbal, will inform you of the expected attire, if not sure just ask. Be sure to pay attention to directives.

In addition to appropriate attire, daily grooming is equally important; a time-honored ritual among men that is easily recognized. It is also quickly noticed when you have not engaged in this important, daily ritual. Grooming includes giving attention to your hair, your face, your mouth, and your body. My nephew, Ryan Hardgraves is a master barber. In the grooming industry, that means he is an expert when it comes to daily appearances. When educating his clients on appearances, Ryan says, "Grooming is a reflection of how we see ourselves. Grooming allows us to develop the confidence to walk into any room with our heads held high because we know we look our best."

A few elements of your grooming ritual should include a regular visit to the barber, including keeping your crown and facial hair under control. Select and regularly use hair and body products that work with your body. Try a few brands until you find what works for you. Make sure you keep the fire in your mouth under control by brushing and flossing at least twice every day. Please take the time to bathe or shower each day with soap and water, not cologne.

I hosted an interest meeting for a group of guys that I eventually mentored. The invitation sent out to the guys clearly stated, "This is a business attire meeting." All but one of the guys showed up in suit and tie or, at least, a shirt and tie. One of the guys did wear a suit and tie, however it looked like he slept in it the night before. Another guy arrived at the meeting in well-ironed jeans and a letterman's jacket and very expensive-looking sneakers. I noticed before the meeting, none of the guys in ties chatted with the one guy in jeans. He became the subject of discussion among some of the other mentors as well.

It dawned on me that both the mentors and the other guys had concluded that either this young man chose to disregard the dress code by wearing jeans and sneakers or he didn't know what "business attire" meant. Either way, it was obvious they decided he was not worthy of inclusion in the pre-meeting conversations. After watching the young man for a minute, it was obvious to him that he was not appropriately dressed. Sidebar: neither the cost of what you are wearing nor the name branded on your outfit excuses you from what is appropriate. This young man failed to understand that every setting has an appropriate and preferred, if not required, attire.

A major part of the mentoring program was to expose young men to new situations; including how to present themselves well with attire and grooming. We spent time learning how to build a wardrobe (a collection of clothing, shoes, belts, etc.) even if there was nothing to begin with. A successful man's wardrobe should include casual items like jeans, chinos, and sneakers. A collection should include business items, starting with a navy suit and a light blue, button-down shirt along with a pair of dark, laced-up oxford shoes. Eventually you want to add formal items, like a tuxedo and a black satin tie.

Sometimes, you have to go to a men's clothing store and ask to be completely fitted. You should know your suit size. Suits come in many sizes in a short (S), regular (R), or long (L) and it is important to remember that suit pants and jeans are not worn the same way. You should know your shirt size; key areas are the neck and the sleeve. Be careful, slim fit is not for thick guys!

You should know your shoe size. Shoes are normally built for narrow, medium, and wide feet. Sidebar: did you know that your two feet are not the same size? Try both shoes on with a dress sock before you buy them. Believe me, the salesperson will be glad to show you. Just be careful they don't persuade you into buying something you really cannot afford at the time. We will talk about managing your money later.

Lessons included how to shave and how to keep their "line" together between haircuts. Like my nephew Ryan, master barbers will teach you how to shave and care for your skin. However, be prepared to pay for such valuable lessons. If not, YouTube has lots of videos. If you are trying to grow your beard, keep the "singleton" hairs trimmed until it has company. Nothing looks worse than a struggling beard.

Each lesson was designed to emphasize the importance of presentation. At home, you're not walking around in a tuxedo. You could, but it's not preferred. At your prom or a big formal event, you're not there looking scruffy in your bathrobe; you probably wouldn't even be allowed in.

The way you dress says whether you know what is acceptable in certain situations or not. You can buy any clothes you want, but keep asking the question,

"Is what I'm wearing appropriate for this situation?" Again, when you are not sure, ask the person who invited you, "What's the attire?" Your first impression is in jeopardy the moment you show up to the party with the wrong clothes. Sidebar: gym gear and flip flops are not appropriate everywhere. While you have the choice to dress the way you choose, not everyone feels the same way you do. The way you dress makes a lasting impression on others. You may forfeit a great opportunity by simply making the wrong attire and grooming choices.

Conversation

Your ability to start and even engage appropriately in a conversation helps you present your best self the first time. The most essential communication skill needed is the ability to engage in a conversation. A conversation is interactive communication between two or more people where thoughts, ideas, and information are exchanged. The purpose of a good conversation is to build a relationship with someone else, whether socially or professionally. A good first conversation leaves a lasting impression about you.

There are basic components to a good conversation. First, make the conversation about the other person, not about you. For example, you may be at a new restaurant and meet the owner or the funders. Remember, when communicating, you must always know the occasion of a conversation, who you are engaging in the conversation with, and your role throughout the conversation.

Next, as we discussed in Chapter 5, be an active listener. Engage in the conversation by actively listening to the owner brag about their new venture; nod your head, smile with your eyes; after all, they invited you to their space. Do not interject anything about your new projects unless asked. If asked, answer with one sentence and turn the conversation back to the owner and their new restaurant.

Flex your conversational skills and move the conversation to a deeper level by asking interesting and open-ended questions. Ask them, "How did you come up with the concept? What's on the menu? What was the hardest part of getting started or when is the best night to come to the restaurant?" Such questions will give you cues for what to talk about next.

Finally, be mindful of the time and space: (think quick introduction, then the longer version). If you are not the only invited guest, the conversation might need to be a quick "hello" and "thank you for the invitation". The owner will appreciate that. The way you engage in a conversation leaves a lasting impression on others.

As a young teacher, especially a Black, male elementary school teacher, I always stood out; there were not many of us at that time. After seeing other Black men in leadership roles, I aspired to be a school administrator. However, I didn't know what to say or what to do in order to become one. After all, I thought I was doing well to become a teacher.

Unbeknownst to me, one of my building principals also thought I would do well as an administrator, so trips to the District Office (DO) were created for me. I got messages during my lunch break saying, "Mr. Seymore, the principal would like for you to pick something up from the DO." At first, I was terrified. There was always an administrator walking in or out of the buildings and they were notorious for smelling the scent of fear coming from the new teachers.

Oddly enough, before each visit, I was called into the main office where the secretary would make sure I was dressed appropriately. I would recite my "elevator speech" to the Assistant Principal and the intent was to make sure I was prepared to present my best self, the first time.

Sidebar: The term "elevator speech" comes from those quick opportunities in Corporate America when aspiring executives (who usually worked in the basement handling mail or answering the phone) would meet a top-level executive on the elevator. This was that small window of opportunity for the "little guy" to introduce themselves to the "big guy." From the moment the elevator doors closed to the time they opened again was all the time the aspiring executives had to introduce themselves and tell what they were all about. If they were impressive enough, the top executive might say "Walk with me and tell me more."

Not only was I terrified about going to the DO, I was terrified I would not represent my principal well. After each visit to the district office, I would have to report with who I met and how the conversation went. A principal told me one of the DO administrators called to speak highly of our brief conversation. My confidence rose and brief introductions became follow up conversations. Before long, I prepared for my own encounters with administrators. To some degree, I credit those "elevator speech" prep session for my promotion to, you guessed it, a building administrator! I have applied that same preparation technique to every situation where I meet someone for the first time and it has yet to fail me.

Opportunity may not always come with prior

notice. Many times, it will come when you least expect it. Regardless of when and how, you must always be prepared to present your best self the first time. Your ability to start and even hold a conversation with others leaves a lasting impression. I challenge you to master the art of conversation. Get in the mirror and practice, practice, practice! Remember, make the conversation more about the other person than yourself. Listen attentively more than you speak. Ask questions that give you cues for how to direct and engage in the conversation. Be mindful of the time and space you're in. Get an "elevator speech". Be prepared for that time when someone says to you, "Tell me about yourself." Again, practice, practice, practice.

When you're invited into a conversation, make sure your "elevator speech" introduces who you are, what your goals in life are, and how you plan to achieve them. When you get the "Tell me more" question, tell them your why. Your intent is to leave a lasting impression.

Body Language

When meeting someone for the first time, your body language or posture can help you present your best self the first time. Posture is the way an individual holds his body to communicate information and the way he feels. For example, crossed arms says you might be hostile or closed off [12]. Lowering your eyes or looking away might communicate you are uninterested or have something to hide. The way you hold your body in the presence of others for the first time leaves a lasting impression.

I had an opportunity to speak with a Black, male, Fortune-500 executive who hosts college-age interns at his company. During our discussion, we talked about his experiences mentoring individuals interested in corporate careers. I narrowed the conversation down and asked him about the toughest things he had to deal with when engaging with his interns. His demeanor was one of hurt and disappointment and I would soon understand why.

The executive explained that, as an African

American male (the only one of his kind there for a very long time), it was important for him to do all he could to create opportunities for other Black men interested in being successful in the profession. In a disappointing tone, he shared that the biggest issue he faced was addressing the way his Black interns' posture was so different from other interns.

He went on to say that young men of color often sat slumped in their seats and held their heads down when talking to him. Whereas the "other" interns stood up straight and looked him directly in the eye when they spoke. The executive shared he could no longer count the number of Black men who never got an interview or call-back because of the impression they make on HR officers. It was clear when it came time to hiring interns for permanent positions, the interns of color usually were not selected. As a result, this executive took it upon himself to "sponsor" a Black male intern at least once a year.

Sidebar: a sponsor is an individual, usually in a position of authority, who volunteers to personally train, mentor ,and guide another individual (mentee) to the next level in their career. A sponsor could go as far as tell their mentee how to sit in a meeting, how to communicate in the work space, or how to get on and off the elevator. The sponsor shows the mentee the ropes. If the mentee follows the guidance of the sponsor, the mentee is usually very successful. In this situation, the rationale for mentoring these interns centered on their body language. This Fortune-500 executive went on to share that in his industry, enthusiasm and confidence are crucial to success, and body language was an essential element to master.

The way you stand when engaging with individuals, especially those you don't know, communicates how much you know about body language. Not everyone gets a sponsor. Most times, simply standing up straight, not slouching when sitting, and looking people in their eyes when talking can help gain immediate respect with peers and authority figures. Being able to control your body's posture makes you a stronger contender to have success with people and in your workplace.

While in office, Barack Obama, the 44th President of the United States, was known for his swag. His unwavering ability to be poised, eloquent, and dashing is why he gained the hearts and respect of Americans. You don't have to become president to possess the kind of swag that gives you power to impress anyone you meet for the first time.

Personal Application

As a man of color, it is important to know there are no days off with your presentation. Every day and every contact you make with another person is an interview.

I used to believe the myth that having a certain swag was reserved for presidents or people of power. I came to understand that I, as L.G. Seymore's grandson, had my own swag!

My grandfather was a well-respected businessman; the owner of an auto repair shop and two gas stations who wore oil-stained overalls during the week.

However, when it was time to "handle business," he put on his Hickey Freeman blazer, perfectly-ironed white shirt, beautiful, shiny shoes, and a matching fedora. With a fresh haircut, he finished the look with a dab of Aramis cologne, what he called "Stankwater." My 5'4" Big Daddy was transformed into "Mr. Seymore." You might say, he was "swagalicious" and he knew it!

With examples like my grandfather and my godfather, I realized that I was a Black man destined for greatness. Therefore, it was my duty to myself and those I represented to start "stepping out correctly." As invitations to fancy meetings with CEOs and School District Administrators quickly came, I didn't have time to "get ready." I needed to always be ready to look like I belonged in the room. I needed to speak like I was a major contributor to the conversation. Likewise, it is your responsibility to present yourself in a way that speaks to your strengths and assets, no matter the age or occupation you hold; you have to take your self-image seriously.

Unfortunately, there are many doors that are not readily open to young men of color who do not come across as polished. As a career educator, the mere fact that I was Black and male could have limited my career advancement and derailed my why. Given the cues from other Black males, I had to learn the difference between streetwear and office attire. I had to learn to engage in conversations in which I was not a subject matter expert. Until I reached a certain level of confidence in myself, I even had to learn to control my raised eyebrow to make sure what I was thinking was not misunderstood.

Opportunities will present themselves to you to be a shining star. When they do, it is important you are prepared to present your best self immediately. Let me be clear; there will be no time to get ready and such opportunities may not come again. Be prepared. I used to hear older men of my community say, "I stay ready so that I don't have to get ready!" This means, always know how to select the appropriate attire and when you don't know, ask questions. Being prepared means practicing what to say in certain situations, even if you do so at the most inopportune time. It means being mindful of your body language. Don't dismiss your greatness before you get to speak.

8

KNOW YOUR
VALUABLE RESOURCES

" The greatness of a man is not how much wealth he acquires, but in his integrity and his ability to affect those around him positively."
-Bob Marley

Recognize The Valuable Things

I was watching a YouTube video and the presenter was talking about knowing your value. He took out a dollar bill, held it up, and asked the audience, "What's the value of this dollar bill? They responded, "One dollar." He folded it, balled it up, stomped on it, and again asked "What's the value now? Again, the audience responded, "One dollar." Then he tore it, poured some unknown liquid on it and threw it in a trash can. Once more, he asked, "What's the value now?"

Before the audience could respond, the presenter shared that in a dumpster, covered with beer, molded food, and goo, this torn, tattered, thrown away dollar, which might not have value to many, may be riches to a homeless person. In fact, it might be more valuable than simply $1.00 because, what if it came in the perfect time of need?

In that moment I realized something important about myself; while I had not been thrown away by others, I, at one point didn't know my own value. I decided since I looked a certain way and had gone through some emotionally damaging things in life, I had little or no value.

While watching the video, a light came on in my mind and I sat bolt upright in bed. It felt like my bedroom turned into one of those commercials with clouds and angels singing "Hallelujah" and in that moment, I realized: God had given me a life and a few experiences that taught me some important lessons. I now possessed unique skills and abilities that made my life better and could make the lives of others better. Those were my resources and those resources were my value.

Every young man of color needs to know his value. The way you perceive your value will affect how other people see you. You have resources within you. You have cultural collateral and alternative capitol. You are bilingual. Those are resources. The problem is some men of color have become apathetic, listening to others downplay who they are. When you know how to use your money, your time, and your talent, you can help yourself, your family, and your community. When used properly, financial literacy, time management, and life-balancing skills increase your value.

Financial Literacy

Money is a resource that, if managed properly, will increase your value. One way to manage money is to become knowledgeable about how it works.. Financial literacy is the ability to understand and effectively use various financial skills and concepts. For example, using a household budget, managing and paying off debt, and evaluating different credit and investment products are financial literacy skills.

I remember getting my first credit card while in college. All of a sudden, I had $1,000 to spend. For someone who had very little, I thought I had arrived! I could go into a store like a "baller" and get what I wanted and boy did I! I bought things for my soon-to-arrive nephew. I bought things for my mother. Of course, buying for others had to be a good thing, right? Then the bill came.

I had two work study jobs and side hustles on the weekend to pay it off. I thought I had it all under control. For months, I would pay the "minimum" required. I thought that gave me a little more to spend. However, instead of the credit card balance going down, it was increasing!

I called the customer service number on the back of the card. A lady with a pleasant voice answered, "This is ABC Customer service. How can I help you?" In my most "educated college voice," I introduced myself and told the representative that my credit limit was $1,000 but my bill was much more. Then I asked why the amount due was increasing, even though I'd been paying the "amount due" each month. Surely, there was an error somewhere.

The representative paused and responded with a long "Well, let me see." I should have known that wasn't good. I was blown away by what the representative called the "annual fees" and "interest rates." She explained that when I signed the contract, the credit card company charged a fee for using the card every year, whether I used the card or not. I interrupted in my mother's voice, "You mean to tell me I was charged for holding this card in my wallet? The representative responded, "Yes." Then she explained each month, an additional fee was added to the bill based on what had not been paid. I would have to pay not only what I used, but the additional fee as well.

By this point, there was a warm sensation rising up from my feet, through my chest, and into my head. Sidebar: when you sign a contract, there is nothing in the fine print that says the customer service representative has to be nice. Your hand (and credit) are in the lion's mouth, so be appreciative when they are kind.

The representative went on to say that the only way to avoid this extra fee was to pay the full amount due before the end of the billing cycle.

Unfortunately, that was the beginning of a terrible cycle of debt in my life. I would go on to use credit to pay for credit. Many young adults make poor financial decisions simply because they don't know that there is good credit and bad credit. Had I known how credit works, I would have made better decisions. Your money is only a resource and an added value to you when you know how to use it.

Time Management

Every second of your time is a resource. When you understand how to use your time properly, you increase your productivity, thus increasing your value. Time management is your ability to use your time effectively or productively at work, at home, or in the community. For example, creating a personal schedule, getting up at the same time each day, and breaking your day into "chunks" are forms of time management.

Managing the resource of time has to be intentional. When something is done on purpose, or deliberately, it's done intentionally. When you manage your time on purpose or deliberately, you are intentionally managing time. For example, when you made a plan to study for a class every day from 1-3 in the afternoon or you deliberately block out time each day to read a book, you are intentionally managing your time. Intentional time management increases your value.

Managing your resource of time requires you to be accountable. The word "accountable" means answerable for actions or decisions. To hold someone accountable means asking the person to explain why they did (or didn't do) something.

Explaining why you did or didn't do something you said you would do is accountable time management. An example of personal time management accountability is when you have someone remind you and make sure you study when you plan too. Being accountable to manage your time increases your value.

In some cases, managing the resource of time causes you to be flexible. Being ready and able to change and show adaptability to different circumstances is flexibility. For example, if you had to push back studying for an hour because you had a flat tire, or you didn't get a chance to read because you were caught by a rainstorm, you are still showing flexibility with your time management. Flexibility in managing your time increases your value. Spend your time with the right people. Spend your time doing things that increase your value. Enjoy the experience without spending the time.

Balanced Life

Your gifts, abilities, and talents (GATs) are resources that increase your value. However, it is critical you balance you "GATs" with the rest of your resources. A balanced life means making sure all aspects of your life get your attention. For example, building relationships along with career advancement is balanced living. Working out and eating healthy, while taking time out to relax your mind, is balanced living.

Growing up, there never seemed to be a surplus

of free time, play time, or even money. It seemed like every day was filled with getting up early for school, doing chores by a certain time, going to bed, and starting over again the next day. I didn't know that this cycle was not productive. Everyone in my neighborhood did the same things. In fact, I thought it was the norm.

I have always been the one to reach for the next level. If it wasn't from one degree to another, it was from one career position to the next. Achievement is wonderful, but if achievement is the priority, there is a cost. Here's what I mean.

When I started the path to my doctoral degree, my sons were still in elementary school. As children of divorce, they traveled a lot between parents. When they traveled to me for weekends, school breaks or vacations, we were not alone. They contended with my books, my articles, and my research.

I remember a time we were at the beach on the Eastern Shore of Maryland. As usual, they found me buried in a book. My younger son clearly wanted my attention but my older son said to his brother, "Be quiet! Daddy is doing his homework." Once I glanced over and saw the disappointment on both of their faces. In that moment, I realized that not only had my studies taken over my spare time, but now it had taken over precious time with my sons. It was important that I shifted gears immediately, and in a big way.

That day, I made arrangements for us to go jet skiing. We were sharing a beach house with friends, so I asked if they would join us so both sons would be on water at the same time with me. They had a blast. Both of them were laughing and smiling the whole time we water skied. As we raced across the lake, the skis nearly turned over, but they laughed anyway. The look on their faces told the story. In that moment, they knew they were the priority. Later that evening, we had dinner and I wasn't surprised when they crashed. They were worn out. My older son crawled up to me on the sofa and told me how much fun he had. In that moment, a small part of me wanted to pull out the books, but I couldn't. The two of them had fallen asleep, one to the left and one to the right of me. That closeness was my signal to leave the books alone and balance my life by holding my sons with affection and attention, rather than always focusing on the next level.

The next morning, my younger son brought my backpack to me. I asked what was he doing and he responded that he knew I needed to get back to my homework, so he was bringing it to me. Again, one part of my life had become so dominant that even my children had conformed to the routine. Instead of taking the backpack and starting to work, I had him take it back to the bedroom. I made arrangements for us to go to the beach for the day. Once there, we encountered a man walking down the beach shouting, "Parasailing anyone?" He had a thick Spanish accent that intrigued my sons and as boys do, they both started mimicking the guy so much we were all folding over in laughter.

As we wiped the tears of laughter from our eyes,

my young son asked, "Daddy, what is parasailing?" Before I could answer, my older son pointed to the brightly colored, kite-looking sails flying in the air with people hanging on them. Instantly, my heart started racing and sweat beads started to form on my brow. I tried to let that conversation fade away. Sidebar: Dr. Sey is, and has always been, afraid of heights. That includes bridges, overpasses, skyscrapers and the like. I had already used up all my courage for the morning driving across the Bay bridge to get there. If you'd seen me on that drive, you'd have laughed at the vision of me driving like a little old lady. Both hands gripping the wheel at a perfect 10 and 2.

I was praying that my two daredevil sons had no interest in parasailing. I was wrong. In less than 30 minutes, we were 1,600 feet in the air.

As we approached the booth to buy tickets, I thought to myself, "Are you crazy?" As I looked down, the boys were pounding their feet like they were about to win something and when I think about it, they were. They were about to win more time with me.

As we got closer to the counter, their smiles grew larger. They were pointing at the sails already in the air, saying to each other, "We are going to go as high as they will allow us." I thought to myself, " No, we are not." When the attendant asked if we wanted the 800-foot lift or the 1,600-foot lift, before I could answer, the boys shouted out, "We want to go up to 1,600 feet!" At that point, I knew there was no turning back.

As we harnessed up, I asked if anyone had changed their minds; you can guess what the answer was. I said a prayer and before I could finish, we were moving. We sat on the back of the boat and in one movement, the boat sped up and we were sliding off the boat. I remember saying to myself, "Well, if we die, we'll all be together." We slowly started rising up to 100-feet, then 500-feet, then 800-feet. I could hear the captain saying, "Here you go to 1,600 feet!" At that point, it really didn't matter, it all felt the same.

While floating high in the air with the Atlantic ocean beneath us, the boys laughed and kicked their feet and waved their hands. In that moment, I kept thinking about how blessed I was to share that experience with them. In that moment, I thought about how those quiet times alone with them would quickly fade away as they grew older. I thought, degrees and promotions were important if I was going to support them, but as they would later share with me when they were adults, the degrees I earned and positions I was promoted too were not important to them. What was important to them was the time we spent together.

As a Black man, your social life is important. Your career aspirations are urgent. However, your family is everything to you. There will be times when family requires more of your time than you want to give. There will be times when you have to work far more hours that you anticipated. There will be times when you want to ball yourself up in a room with your PS4 for two days just to unwind from the stress. Each of those areas of your life are urgent and important. However, in order to have a happy and fulfilling life, there has to be balance between what you want to do, what you love to do, and what you need to do. Just remember that there is only one you. You can't be everything to everyone. You must create balance.

Personal Application

In Chapter 1, we talked about our mental state. In the earlier chapters of our life, many of us feel like because of what we have gone through, because we didn't come from the right neighborhood, we don't have value. The truth is, we have great value. However, it is within us and it is our responsibility to recognize our own value and the resources we bring to the table.

We talked earlier about how my grandfather and godfather were men of great integrity. I shared how they were both men of great faith and very family oriented. What I didn't share was that I was awestruck by these men and these influences changed me forever.

9

KNOW MORE THAN YOUR NEIGHBORHOOD

"The world is my classroom, each day is a new lesson, and every person I meet is my teacher."
-Craig Harper

Beyond the Block

There's a wonderful organization named "My Block, My Hood, My City." This organization takes teens from Chicago's urban communities and shows them places around the city. Every month, the teens visit different neighborhood business centers, restaurants, museums, and other destinations. The idea is to visit places outside of their communities that they ordinarily would not go. The intent of the explorations is to empower youth to explore new places, experience new things, and evolve into new beings that poverty and isolation might not afford or even allow for them.

For many guys like you and I, the block on which we live has framed the way we see and think about the world. Here's what I mean. Most of the things that we need to survive are right around us. Our family and friends are close. They live in the same building, down the block, or around the corner. Schools, church, the "stoe," and little league are no further than a few streets down from our front doors. The parties and events we get invited to are within walking distance, or no further than a 15-minute ride in a car. Few people we know have traveled to other states, so often, our conversations and points of reference are about "the hood." As a result, most of us learn to live and survive in a limited space called, "my block." Our thinking is much the same.

We only think about what our present situation has to offer us. We convince ourselves that "This is the way it's going to be." Unfortunately, when we do leave our neighborhood, it is difficult to function comfortably because we simply don't have the experiences of being or thinking past the corners that framed our lives.

Let me tell you, there is so much out there, so much to do, so much the big world has to offer. The only way you get to see it or experience new things is to give yourself permission to travel. In the article that highlighted "My Block, My Hood, My City," the Manhattan Institute for Poverty Research talks about the real impact of travel. In short, travel ignites curiosity. Once you find out it's nice to visit downtown, you'll be curious to visit more. Travel drives ambition. Once you see there are people that look like you doing great things on the other side of town, you're going to want to want to "Be somebody when you grow up." Travel leads to success. The more you travel past the limits of your immediate community, the more likely you are willing to travel past the limits of your imagination. The more you travel to different places, the more you learn. The more you discover about the "outside world," the more you'll want to know.

When I was about 11 or 12, I took organ lessons. Once each week, my mother and I would get on the bus and travel to Brook Mays Music on Main Street. Brook Mays Music was an old Houston establishment. I never saw others that looked like me patronizing this business. Inside, there were shiny black pianos and white pianos on one side of the showroom and organs of all sizes on the other. When you walked through the showroom to the music studio, the temptation was always there; to touch, to listen, to explore. Initially, I think one of the salesmen could sense my curiosity because he would always say, "Try it out." In the back of my head, I could hear my mother saying, "you'd better not!" However, I could sense my mother's opposition. Sidebar: I grew up in one of those households where every time we went somewhere, you were reminded of the law, "Don't touch anything you were not buying!" Week after week, I never saw anyone that looked like me. There were no Black sales persons. There were no Black customers. There were no other Black music students. Each week, I felt like I did not belong in this place. However, I later realized that my mother was in some way saying, "You have talent. You belong here, even if you're the only one." To some degree, after I touched the first key on that baby grand piano and no alarms went off, nobody told me I could not allow my natural curiosity to take over, I knew I belonged.

I loved music, but I hated taking organ lessons.

Strange right? I grew up loving the sound of Marching Bands, especially when I knew the music they played. The band at Francis Scott Key Junior High was next door to my elementary school, J.C. McDade. Key Jr. High, the "Old Kashmere High School" was renowned for its football and basketball teams, and more important to me, its award-winning band. It was a community fixture. The band director was Mr. Turner. Every evening before football practice, he had band on the field, marching and playing. Man, that music was off the chain! I remember missing the school bus home so I could listen to them play the latest in R&B. If I timed it right, I could listen to roughly 15-minutes of music and still get home before my mother's daily call from work. There was something about the horns, the drumline, and the tuba sections playing music by the Jackson Five and the OJays that made the bystanders want to dance. Eventually, I took a music class in middle school, but I never made the band.

The primary reason I disliked organ lessons was

because of the music I was being taught to play. I was learning "Oh When the Saints Go Marching In" and "Michael Row Your Boat Ashore". Those were clearly not what I was accustomed to. Sidebar: Every Saturday morning, our black-and-white television was tuned in to Mr. Don Cornelius and the "Sooooul Train". To make matters worse, my cousin Dana was also taking music lessons, but she was playing music by the Clark Sisters!"

Every time Dana visited, we would have to play for the adults and I hated it. I would play something that I had learned while Dana would play "Is My Living in Vain". In my village, gospel and R&B were THE music jargons. If you could play either of those well, you were doing something. At that age, I didn't know or care about all that research mumbo-jumbo that said learning music would help me perform better academically. All I thought was "This is so boring."

While I didn't like the music lessons, the lessons I learned during those three hours outside of my neighborhood would last a lifetime.

Every trip was both entertaining and informative. On my way to music lessons, the "6-Jensen" bus would pass the street pharmacy, where Lenny was always open for business and the ladies recessed in scant, brightly-colored dresses, smiling and posing like runway models in the middle of the street. If the bus driver had to stop for a prolonged period, the men in the fancy cars would stop to talk to the ladies. Little did I know, they were prostitutes and "Johns" but to me, the impression was strong. The Po-Po were always giving someone a hard time. For a time, I thought the police only worked on my side of town. Once I ventured out of my own neighborhood, the world seemed like a totally different place.

In addition to music lessons allowing me to travel outside of my neighborhood, it also afforded me sacred bonding time with my Mama. On a specific day, for a few hours, I didn't have to share my mother with the rest of the family, or the daily grind of life. It was always our time. That one evening each week, I had her all to myself. I never thought I would grow up. I never imagined my interests would change and I would need to be more independent, but Mama knew. Up to this point, most of the influencers I've mentioned in this book have been the men of my village, but I would be remiss if I did not mention the tantamount influence my mother had on my life. She insisted that, among so many other life lessons, I learn how to navigate the world outside of my neighborhood.

Since those adventure-filled days with my mother, I have concluded that since many young males of color grew up with fathers, who themselves may have not been equipped for fatherhood, or for whatever reason, chose not to assume parental responsibilities, mothers are usually the ones to make it happen. Thus, my mother gets all the credit for my curiosity about the world. It probably explains my spending 20 years of living in practically every geographic region of the country and why I have such an adventurous spirit. While the males in my life taught me how to "be," my mother taught me how to explore. I think she knew that I was going to find my way outside of Fifth Ward, and even Texas. So she taught me how to "belong" in whatever place I was at any given time.

Since I'm writing from a male's perspective, I feel comfortable sharing this statement: I get so annoyed when I hear someone say, "A woman can raise her son to be a man." Or another one that really gets me is, "Happy Father's Day to all the single mothers!"

I think women do phenomenal jobs of being awesome mothers, especially when they have to parent single-handedly. They do a miraculous job of making sure that a "knuckle-head" is well-mannered and respectful. I like to think Mary Seymore-Walker did a fairly decent job herself. But no matter how fierce, a lioness cannot be a lion. Likewise, a mother cannot be a father. As a son, a father, and a mentor to young Black males whose fathers, for whatever reason, did not play significant roles in their lives, let me be clear. There are just certain things a boy has to be taught by a man and how to be a man is the most important lesson.

Time after time, I have witnessed young men earning compliments for being well- mannered and respectful, but when that same young man grows up and doesn't see the need to move out of his mother's house, guess who is the first to complain? When this adult son has no clue of what it means to plan a life or to take care of a family, he is crucified by the same people who laid out the commendations.

A male cub learns to stand tall and strong, to hunt and protect his pride by watching other, male lions. Remember The Lion King? Even as a cub, Simba mimicked his father, Mufasa's roar. When Simba drinks from the river, he sees his father's reflection. Boys growing into men seek validation first from their fathers, even if he's not present.

There is some validity to the cliché that implies men and women are from different planets. Men see the world differently than women. Whether good or bad, boys learn to be men from other men. A great mother, who teaches her son to be well-mannered and respectful, should also seek out good role models for her son when his father is not present.

To all the young brothers who have taken on their mother's negative feelings about their biological fathers, be careful. It is possible, in her mind, you become the man you have practiced disliking (from her influence) all your life. Before you know it, you hear, "You're just like your father." Remember, there are three sides to every story. There's his side, her side, and the truth. You get to decide what kind of man you want to be.

Each time my mother and I would go out for music lessons, she would give me explicit instructions for how to behave and what to do. "Always do this and pay attention to that," she would say. Mother would always include, "You might have to do this on your own one day." I rarely paid that part any mind.

Most times, my imagination was in overdrive. My attention would be on all the buildings, so tall you couldn't see the top floor from the window of the bus. I was fascinated by people of all shapes, sizes, and colors, always coming and going somewhere. The bus would always stop at the Foley's department stores. Each week, there would be a different suit and shoes on the mannequins. There were certainly no fancy stores and tall buildings like this in my neighborhood. The bus passed the big corporate office buildings like Tenneco Oil and First Trust Bank. Occasionally, I would see men that looked like me leave the tall offices to get in their fancy cars at the end of the day. While they weren't traveling toward my neighborhood, I often wondered why they dressed like they did and drove cars like they drove, what kind of houses they lived in. Wherever they lived, I wanted to live there too.

Some days, Mama would have me tell her which bus we should take. Other days, she would have me pull the cord to signal the bus driver that we had reached our stop. I'm certain this was her way to make sure I was paying attention to her navigation lessons. I remember asking Mama what would happen if we got on the wrong bus or missed our stop. She would shrug her shoulders and look away. A few times when we did get on the wrong bus and even passed our stop. We would have to walk several blocks back to the music studio. My Mama was a short stout woman. So making our way along the busy concrete of the downtown streets of Houston midsummer was no walk in the park. I don't remember making such mistakes too often because there was an urgency for me to know how to get where I was going and back home safely. In those trips, my Mama taught me how to be self-sufficient.

We always had to take two buses to the music studio; first the 6 Jensen, then the South Main-Medical Center. There was a McDonald's about midway downtown. It was the landmark we used as the place to transfer from one bus to the next. Each week, I looked forward to transferring there because we would always stop for dinner on the way home. Sidebar: our standard of living was very lean. There was no such thing as disposable income and every penny counted. Eating out was always a big deal. I later learned that Mama would not have lunch on those days so I could have McDonald's for dinner. Her selfless sacrifices are why I honor her to this day.

While having dinner at the Main Street McDonald's, there were always people coming and going. Some of them looked like me and others didn't. Mama told me many of the people lived far away and would be late getting home and this was where they stopped in to get a quick bite to eat. Back then, it was strange that these people, who shared the same twelve or so square blocks for nine hours each day, would depart, going in different directions. But the next day, they simple pressed repeat.

My mother pointed out that it was important to pay attention to how the different people carried themselves. I noticed that there were men and women who didn't look like me. I was always drawn to those who did. There was something about them that showed they were comfortable with everyone around them. They smiled. They spoke very clearly. They exuded confidence. They always had a briefcase in their hand and a newspaper under their arm. To me, that meant, regardless of the life they lived, they were informed, and "about their business." Mama would always say, "Whether or not people are dressed a certain way or they talk a certain way, everyone in here wants to do better."

After a few months, I had to put into practice all those navigation lessons she taught me on those summer days. I had to prove myself. Mother trusted me to take the bus from home to music lessons and back, all alone. Back then, there were phones anyone could use for only $0.25, usually located on every other corner and there was a pay phone just outside the music studio door. Every day, my mother's instructions were to call home the minute I stepped off the bus to say I had arrived. Then, I had to call immediately after lessons were over to say I was on my way home. Back then, you could calculate the time it took to get from one place to another, down to the minute. Unfortunately, I was not allowed to stop and have dinner at McDonald's, but I was allowed to grab a drink to go, as long as I didn't miss the bus. One missed call or missed bus could have been the end of my newly found independence

After some time of riding the same bus to and from the same location, I started to become familiar with the people who rode the same buses and always sat on the same seats. I enjoyed feeling like a part of the people who were "all about their business."

One day, a lady asked me where I was going every day with my music folder. I remember telling her I was going to take music lessons downtown. She responded with a big smile her face. After the first conversation, she saved a seat for me every day, right next to her. At first, we talked about what music piece I was going to play that day and how I hated it. Then, we had conversations that lasted the whole ride about all the places that one bus could take me if I ever wanted to see more of the city. As time passed, I learned to take the bus all over the city of Houston. Even then, it was a big place. Man! There were so many places to see and so much to learn. I planned to learn them all.

I stopped taking music lessons after a year, but one thing I remember the lady saying was "Keep up the good work. You're going to be somebody one day."

Had I not taken music lessons outside of my neighborhood, I probably never would have learned how to function in places different from and outside of my neighborhood. I would not have developed a desire to see what other places that one city bus could take me. I would have never learned how to engage with people who didn't look like me, function in places that made me uncomfortable, or try things I had never tried.

Every young man of color needs to know how to navigate outside of his neighborhood. According to Forbes, traveling to new places whether far or near, reduces stress, boosts happiness and satisfaction, and makes you mentally resilient [10] . A neighborhood is a place with familiar faces and behaviors that makes us comfortable but young men need to know how to engage with other cultures, how to rise in uncomfortable settings, and how to remain open to new experiences.

So often, Black men are marginalized to such a degree that we have become complacent in "our place." In reality, every place is "our place." The seven deadly words we use which have always kept Black men marginalized are "I have always done it that way."

Our neighborhood is a safe place, yet it can harbor apathy and stifle our capacity for growth. It is good to be a strong, confident Black man in spaces that are not accustomed to seeing us. In fact, many cultures are starting to realize that the narrative of Black men has been misconstrued. Many of the optics have been intentionally orchestrated to depict us as either lazy, with no ambition, or angry and violent. Oddly enough, other cultures want to know who Black men are, but are "uncomfortable" asking. Due to " fragility" misinformation, other cultures are careful not to "say the wrong thing" around Black men. When you know how to navigate outside of your neighborhood, you come to appreciate your own identity. You broaden your perspective of the world and the world's understanding of you. When you don't, you remain confined to the borders of your imagination and the world remains misinformed about the qualities a Black man brings to any situation. There are several ways you can find your way outside of your neighborhood.

One way to function outside of what is comfortable to you is to expose yourself to different places and cultures. Here's what I mean. Think about your last trip away from home. Where did you go? What did you do ? What other foods did you eat? Most likely, you traveled somewhere you've gone before, perhaps to a relative's house. You probably did the same things you always do, going to the mall, eating the same foods you always eat. If I am right, you need to change that. When you expose yourself to different places and cultures, who knows what could happen.

I remember going to my first Caribbean Festival; I was never so amazed as I was at all the things I saw.

That Saturday morning, I ate, got dressed, and took the bus to downtown Houston to the stop closest to the designated festival area. Earlier, I mentioned riding the bus to music lessons and how the bus prompted me to explore other places around the city. However, this area, though not far from Main Street, was not a place I was familiar with. As I got off the bus, I could hear the sounds of metal drums and smell the aroma of food in the air. I didn't know what to expect, but I grew more and more anxious to get there.

When I approached the barricades surrounding the festival, I saw people in all sort of bright colors, laughing and dancing to the music. There were stages scattered throughout the area and food vendors at the far end. The food was stationed strategically at the end of the area so you had to pass all of the stages, craft vendors, and the people to get what you wanted to eat and I noticed then how clever that was.

As I walked toward the food, I passed through a group of people dancing when suddenly, someone grabbed my arm. Immediately, I became defensive. After all, where I was from, when a stranger grabbed your arm, you responded with a fist! Little did I know, at that time, it was customary to include everyone, including and especially strangers, in the celebration dance. Sidebar: remember when I told you that I didn't make the marching band? It was because I couldn't dance.

Not all Black men dance, but in the spirit of camaraderie (and so I didn't look like a stick in the mud), I joined in. After all, I didn't recognize anyone; nobody I knew would see my three left feet in action.

After the impromptu dance in the street, I stumbled upon the crafter's painting people's faces. I tried to slide by without being noticed. But the painters were skilled in picking out apprehensive bystanders. Before I knew it, I had green and white paint on my face, a feather apron around my waist, and I was dancing again with people I didn't know! I thought to myself, "What in the world are you doing?" But the impulse was so strong, I continued to adapt.

Without knowing it, I was navigating another culture. I was surely not going to find any of this type of activity in my neighborhood. At the end of the day, my hands were filled with bags of masks, hats, and other memorabilia. As I headed for home, I reminisced and knew I'd had one of the best times of my life. I had danced with people I didn't know. I had my face painted. I had been in a different world, surrounded by strangers, danced freely and with joy, and all without leaving my city.

Another way to operate outside of your comfort zone is to engage with people who are different from you. For example, take a look at your social media pages. Do you have an Instagram, Facebook, and LinkedIn account? Are all of your friends and contacts your age, gender, and same ethnic background? Are there any from other cultures? If not, you can change that. When you engage with different people, you not only come to understand them more, but they come to understand, first-hand the essence of a Black man.

I remember attending my first Academic Dean's conference. I was so excited; for the first time, I would be in the company of others that do what I do every day. This was an opportunity for me to learn from the experts but I was aware that my experiences would shape the way I saw myself in spaces where I was the only one who looked like me.

The conference was held on one of the largest college campuses in Arkansas. I drove around, trying to find the designated parking area but because students were out on break, there were few people available to help. When I walked into the center, I instinctively looked at the pictures and plaques on the wall. I was looking first to see if there were any Black faces and then, if by chance, I knew them. To my disappointment, there were no Black faces on any of the thousands of pictures and plaques throughout the building.

After my self-guided tour, I found my way to the registration desk. A Caucasian woman greeted me with a smile and said, "Hello. You must be The Dr. Seymore." I responded that I was, but in the back of my head, I wondered, "What did she mean, THE Dr. Seymore?" Was my name so unique that I stood out? Was there someone attending or affiliated with the conference that knew me? This was odd, but I quickly discovered her meaning.

When I opened the registration packet, there was an agenda, a folder with materials for the conference, and a name badge. The name badge had my full name, the name of my university, and a color headshot of me. I didn't think much of the picture. Many salespeople practice this when they are about to meet with a new client whom they've never seen; it minimizes awkward moments of mistaken identities. I put the name badge on and walked into the meeting room. The room slowly filled with Caucasian men and woman and even some Black women. Many joined me at the table where I was seated and each time someone came to the table, they seemed to be overdoing their greeting.

At the top of the hour, the Dean presiding over the conference approached the podium while those facilitating the session closed the doors. Typically, this is an indication that the meeting was about to start, so I took one last glance around the room. Every Black woman whose eyes I met nodded with a smile and suddenly it hit me.

I remember thinking to myself, "Ahh! There is it," I am not only "the Dr. Seymore," I'm also "the Black man" in the room."

The bible offers the scenario of a runner in an arena, preparing to run a race, surrounded by a cloud of witnesses. Those witnesses are ancestors who have run the race before and are now there to cheer the runner on. The scenario goes on to suggest that in order to successfully run (and win) the race, the runner has to take off anything that distracts him. In that moment, I sensed the presence of my grandfather, my godfather, my former pastor, and the deceased men of my community and fraternity surrounding the walls of the room. Dressed in fine suits and ties, with their hats in their hands. I could hear them saying, "We know. We've been the only ones in the room too, but, we are here with you. We are here to cheer you on."

I could feel their hands on my shoulders, squaring them, forcing my chest to expand; strong hands, pushing me in the back, reminding that I should sit tall. I could hear my godfather's voice, loud in my ear saying, "Speak with confidence." I could feel my grandfather crossing my left leg over my right leg, exuding a sense of confidence, a statement that I belonged in the room.

In that moment, my discomfort eased. In session after session, discussions erupted about the plight of Black men in education. Because I was in a room of highly educated administrators, it would have been foolish to speak on a subject from a secondary experience when a Black man was present. I felt the strong hands of those before me and spoke with courage, from experience. Some of my responses confirmed what people in the room thought; other responses left some in awe, as evidenced by their red faces. In each session, any Black woman present gave that non-verbal signal which suggested I had made them proud.

Life has a way of tossing us into an arena. Many times, we are thrown into arenas to fight with lions and bears. We are expected to show up in our full selves. As a Black man, we are expected to rise. To this day, I still get excited about that conference experience. Not only did I find the courage to rise to a herculean challenge, I also found a new confidence in who I am.

As we discussed in Chapter two, we stand on broad shoulders. I stood on broad shoulders that week. I stood on the shoulders of men who had faced racism with dignity at a time when their manhood was challenged and humanity questioned.

Despite the fact I was the only Black man in a space where others like me were not always welcome, I know I contributed to a new level of understanding and respect for Black men just by commanding my own presence in that room. This experience laid the groundwork for my responses to other similar experiences.

Personal Application

I needed to be uncomfortable to become comfortable in that room. I challenge you to be uncomfortable. Put yourself in spaces that make you uncomfortable. Meet people who don't look like you. Speak, even if you don't know what to say the first time you're in the room. There's a cloud of witnesses cheering you on.

The worst thing that could happen is you grow. You learn how to handle yourself and teach others how to handle you.

Dr. Marrix D. Seymore Sr.

10

KNOW HOW TO HELP SOMEONE ELSE

"The secret to being happy is doing things for other people."
-Dick Gregorys

The Importance of Contributing to your Community

In 2018, basketball superstar Lebron James, along with the James Family Foundation, opened a new school in his former community of Akron, Ohio. The I Promise School is a public school and was designed to provide academics as well as social and emotional support to at-risk students. This means Akron taxpayers fund the school and its daily operation, but The James Family Foundation pays for the wraparound service and programs.

Rising third and fourth grade students (averaging 1-2 years behind their peers in reading) were randomly selected from all Akron public schools to attend. At I Promise, tuition, uniforms, and transportation are free, as are meals and snacks during the school day. Every student has access to a fitness trainer, a free bicycle, and a helmet. I Promise students also get a free Chromebook.

The school day starts at 9 a.m. and ends at 5 p.m., with an extended school year starting in July and ending in May. During a seven-week summer session, the I Promise School provides STEM-based camps, where students spend time on social-emotional learning and participate in a "supportive circle" which helps them refocus after lunch. If they complete the school program successfully and graduate from high school, Lebron James covers their full tuition at a local public college, the University of Akron.

In 2019, LeBron helped build transitional housing for families whose children attended the I Promise School, as many families experience homelessness or struggle to have stable, safe housing. In addition, The James Family Foundation offers GED courses and job placement for parents.

Lebron knows what it's like to be an at-risk student himself. As a fourth grader, he says he missed 83 days of school while he and his mother moved from one couch or spare room to the next. He credits mentors, some of whom he met at school, with a turnaround that helped him attend every day of fifth grade - the first year he played organized basketball.

All of the opportunities afforded to I Promise students and their families are driven by James' mission to help kids overcome what he faced as a low-income student in Akron.

Lebron James has won four NBA championships and four league-MVPs, but Lebron still sees the school opening as the greatest moment of his career. He understood the need his community had for quality education, access to services outside of the typical school environment, and safety. Lebron also knew he had resources such as his name and influence, business savvy, and money to make a positive, life-long impact in his community.

Do you Know How to Pay if Forward?

Every man of color needs to know how to contribute to his community. He needs to know how to pay forward what he has been afforded. Everything you are able to do, every place you are able to live, and everything you are able to buy is because of the countless efforts of someone before you. It is true: "We are our ancestors' wildest dreams." By ancestors, I do mean those who endured slavery through the strength of their endurance. I mean those who suffered violence and abuse with resilience and purpose, but I also mean those whose untimely deaths have led to protests which declare: Black lives do matter in America and the world.

Let me be clear: giving back to your community is a choice. You choose to either be an asset or a liability. There is no middle ground. If you do not choose to give your time, talent and/resources to your community, you are making a choice to take from it.

Many Black men feel because they do not have a lot of money, they have nothing to give. One the contrary, we all have something to give. In fact, each of us was built with gifts and abilities to give something of ourselves to make life for another person even better. In Matthew, chapter 25 of the Holy Bible, a passage teaches about using "talents," or, gifts and abilities. In the passage, a man is going on a journey for some time. He leaves all of his property in the care of three of his servants. He gives them all different amounts, based on what they were able to manage. The expectation was that each of them would use their ability to increase what they had been given. The passage doesn't mention their ages, but I like to believe that at any age, we can use what we have been given to contribute to our communities. While the master is away, two of the servants use what they had been given charge of and doubled its amount, showing industriousness. However, one servant chose to hide his talents. He chose to do nothing with what he was given.

When the master returns, he finds that two of the servants invested what they had been given, doubling its value, and as a result, rewards them for their efforts. However, the value of what the third servant had been given remained the same because he did nothing with it. He tried to justify his choices, but the explanation did nothing to ease the master's anger. The master took his property from that servant, gave it to one of the other servants, and sent the third servant away. The master declared that anyone who uses what they have been given will get more, but those who don't use what they have will lose it. Like the servants, all of us have been given gifts and abilities. We are expected to use them to not only to improve our own lives, but to also contribute to the lives of those around us and those who will come after us. There are several ways to do so right where you are, with what you have right now. We can contribute through outreach, community service, and philanthropy.

Do You Know How to Get Involved Through Community Outreach?

One way to contribute to your community is through outreach. Outreach is an activity outside your normal line of work to provide services to any population that might not otherwise have access to those services. Outreach is not stationary, but mobile; in other words, it involves meeting someone in need of an outreach service at the location where they are. For example, outreach includes building a website for a community nonprofit at little to no charge, making sure seniors have access to healthcare via the internet or their phones, and making sure young boys can connect with safe after-school programs, both in-person and virtually.

Earlier in the book, we talked about legacy and how the good things you and your family do to improve the lives of others becomes your legacy. My family's legacy of outreach started long before I was even a thought.

My grandparents moved to Houston, Texas in the mid 1950s from southcentral Louisiana. Over time, they grew their family from one daughter (my mother) to another daughter and two sons. They launched several businesses, as Gramps was always about "hustling" for his family. If men are hunters and gatherers and women are nurturers, my grandfather hunted and gathered the broken and my grandmother nurtured them back to wholeness.

One day, according to my grandmother, my grandfather sent a young man to their house. He had met the young man a few times at the gas station. But after engaging with him, Gramps realized he was homeless. During those days, the Black community was very close-knit. Nobody went hungry or slept in the streets. Gramps promised Granny he would not send any more people to her for help. Needless to say, he didn't keep his promise. At the same time, as was common practice for Black families, some of my grandmother's younger siblings migrated from Louisiana to Texas. They too would spend short stays with my grandparents, which meant any extra space, food, clothing, or attention my mother was accustomed to having, was limited.

My grandmother's name is Nora. As the story goes, my mother took out one of my grandmother's "good white sheets" and painted "Nora's Mission" on it in protest. Sidebar: back in those days, and even now, there were regular sheets the family used every day, then there were "good" sheets for the holidays when company visited.

As far back as I can remember, the "good

white" sheets were never to be slept on or used for any other purpose, except to cover the dining room table. From what I was told, my mother got the worst beating ever for two reasons: first, because she painted on the sacred sheets and second, because she was sarcastic and inhospitable. Granny laid down the law, again, and taught my mother an important lesson: space, food, clothing and even attention was just what my grandparents did for others. If there was a need, it was their duty to meet it.

In our own individual ways, that lesson has been the mantle passed down to generations of Seymore's. If you have it, share it. If you give it, give it with no expectation. I can't tell you how many times I heard the statement, "Unto whom much is given, much is required."

You can help someone regardless of what's in your bank account. There is always a need in your community: it might be something as simple as stopping to say hello to someone confined to their home, or inviting someone to live in your extra space until they can get on their feet again. Reaching out to meet the needs of others is an act which requires intentionality. My grandparents were not rich: they were middle class folk trying to earn a decent living and instill values in their children. Along the way, they recognized they could use what they had to reach out, to help others, and to help themselves in the process.

Community service is another way to contribute to your community. Community service is unpaid work done by a person or group of people that benefits children, senior citizens, people with disabilities, English language learners, and more. It is usually organized through local groups, like a church, a school, or a non-profit organization, to improve places, such as a local parks, historic buildings, or scenic areas. Much like outreach, examples of community service include volunteering at a shelter, organizing a clothing drive, or cleaning up abandoned yards and local areas so children and seniors will be safe.

I left for college in the Fall of 1987. Each year, my family gathered at my grandparents' house for a big Thanksgiving Dinner. Every year, we had turkey, ham, dressing, potatoes, tomatoes, greens, beans: as Pastor Shirley Caesar would say, "U NAME IT," we had it. I often brought friends with me when I came home. For the most part, it was so my mother could meet my friends and my grandmother could cook for them. Thanksgiving was no different.

There were students I knew well and those I'd recently met who could not be with their families for both Thanksgiving and Christmas. Back then, Black college students were broke: we didn't have lots of money and new cars, like many students do today. For the holidays, we piled up in my hooptie (aka old rusted car and bald tires), sometimes seven or eight deep, and went to Granny's. After all, I was raised to meet a need if I saw it and besides, we were just that kind of folk. Everybody had a place and a meal.

While home with me for Thanksgiving, my friends saw how the Seymore's gathered around a table, but they would also see the other guests and friends gathered as well. There were two rules at my grandfather's table: 1. No one was ever turned away, and 2. Children ate first. Over time, my friends would see less emphasis on elaborate meals and more emphasis on making sure this elderly person was fed or that person confined to their home had a meal.

Just as preparing a great feast was a family affair, so was taking care of the needy. Instead of watching us scurry to our favorite places at the table, my friends saw us scurry to our cars to get food delivered by a certain time (Granny insisted that food be delivered hot). By the time I graduated, the traditional dinner had been cancelled and another had begun which evolved into a daily lunch program.

From a takeout restaurant to a shelter for homeless veterans, 6205 Jensen Drive, or as we dearly called it, "The Place," became a seven-day community service clearing house. Instead of food for profit or giving away two to three holidays a year, over 400 people were served hot meals at least three days each week. Annual clothing drives turned "The Place" into a daily collection and giveaway site. To see the operation in full gear was nothing less than a miracle.

As the need for food grew in the community and resources became more and more scarce, my grandparents decided that the family would expand the annual Thanksgiving turkey giveaway to include a Christmas and Easter food giveaway. Days after those events, there were still individuals asking if there was anything left. Before we knew it, food was being given away almost every day of the week. There were food donations from individuals, small groups, and large restaurants. The night before, there were people chopping veggies and basting meat. On the "lunch day," you could find people in the kitchen volunteering to cook and serve food. Granny's philosophy was "Whatever the Lord sends to this driveway, I am going to put it on a plate." It was not surprising to see prime rib on a place one day and chicken cordon bleu another. Each covered plate was served with love and a "God Bless you." Each person that received a meal responded with a "Thank you." In many cases, individuals in line became volunteers themselves. A proud moment for my grandparents was when Granny received the Mayor's Volunteer Award.

After graduation, my friends from college became adopted family members. We would reminisce about how my family always had some kind of community effort going for the needy. They would always ask, "Why did your grandparents do so much for others?" Some would point out how later generations were still heavily involved in community service today. When asked, any family member would simply respond, "That's just what we do."

You can start or participate in a community service project. When my grandparents acted on a drive to help those in need, it encouraged others to help. In the meantime, some of those who helped found passion projects of their own. Goodwill is like a grain of sand that rolls down a hill: the more it rolls, the larger and stronger it gets. A desire to help other people led my grandparents to a specific group of people who needed ongoing help but it was their courage to do something which led them to their life's work.

You can contribute to your community through philanthropy. Philanthropy is often defined as giving gifts of "time, talent and treasure" to help make life better for other people. For example, making a monetary gift to a cause you believe in, serving in a soup kitchen, tutoring a teen, or engaging in any other volunteer activity is philanthropy. The main idea is giving to improve lives.

In 1998, my grandparents, a retired mechanic and registered nurse, started Caring Heart Outreach Ministries. Caring Heart's mission was to meet the physical, emotional, and spiritual needs of individuals who were either homeless or very close to living without the basic needs of life. Their work targeted homeless veterans, men who had served in the military but found themselves down on their luck.

My grandparents were already familiar with

offering food and shelter to the masses. They'd taken care of family members and who knows how many strangers-turned-friends over the years. I remember my grandmother always quoting my grandfather as saying, "With a nickel, a nail and the Lord, we can make it happen. Now let's go to work!" They used their retirement savings and repurposed a small building into a shelter for veterans. They sought help from community agencies to find "fresh start" resources for veterans. Oddly enough, the more veterans they helped, the more agencies wanted to help them.

There was a purpose for this work: the idea was that these men would someday get back on their feet. While my grandfather took care of the facilities, my grandmother made sure each resident was actively doing what he needed to do. The other side of my grandmother was that she could not tolerate adult men feeling down on themselves and not doing anything about it. She too was one of those who subscribed to the notion that failing is ok, as long as you keep trying.

Each day, the residents had to have a daily plan for getting their lives together. Either they were going to some development program, looking for a job, or they were volunteering in the community. Each tenant had assigned duties around the shelter, designed to prepare them to take care of themselves once they were on their own again. At the end of each day, there was a hot, home-cooked meal, prepared by my grandmother. Over time, this tough, no- nonsense lady went from being called Mrs. Seymore to Mama Seymore by the tenants.

Through this work, many veterans were able to reconnect with lost families and reestablish themselves in society. As a part of the giving forward message of my grandparents and the organization, several of the veterans we cared for either started their own work to help homeless veterans or started working for the Veteran's Administration in some manner.

You can be a philanthropist regardless of how

many resources (or how few) you have. Find a cause that is important to you. Do the research and find out what's been done already. There is always a niche or a space that needs to be filled. Knock on some doors, ask questions, start doing something. The more you do for others, the more others will want to help you; it's the principle of sowing and reaping. My grandparents started meeting a need for the homeless. They found out there was a greater need for a specific group of people. The more they wanted to help veterans, the more others wanted to help them.

Think about the last time someone did something for you for no reason and expected nothing in return. Now, think about if that something happened for you in the nick of time and you don't know who did it, or why? How did that make you feel? I don't know how you felt, but for the person who helped you, I know firsthand, it made them feel like they did the right thing. I am certain that they may have not had much, but they saw a need and attempted to meet it.

People always thought my grandparents were rich and in a sense, they were. They didn't have much money, but they were very resourceful. They didn't mind using what they had to help others. I remember my grandfather saying many times that if you see a man who needs a pair of shoes, buy him a pair and don't talk about it. If you can't afford to buy him shoes, give the ones on your feet and don't complain about it. You have far more than he does. I practice that very thing to this day. Yes, I have given the very shoes off my feet to someone in need. My grandparents used their personal resources of a good name, influence, and some retirement money to impact an entire community. They turned their passion into the last jobs either of them would have.

Personal Application

You don't have to be Lebron James. You don't have to be my grandparents, or anyone else. However, because I know at some time in your life, someone did something for you, now, you MUST pass it on. I challenge you to find a way to give back to your community. Look around and ask yourself, "What's missing?" Then, find a way to fill that gap. Knock on doors, ask questions, reach out further than your family or friends to help. I have to warn you though, service to others is an addiction! When done for the right reasons, the more you do, the more you will want to do.

"Service is the rent you pay for your room here on Earth."
-Mahammad Ali

MEET THE AUTHOR

Dr. Seymore is an advocate of self-improvement at any age, in any situation. He earned a Bachelor of Science degree in Elementary Education and a Master of Education degree in Administration Leadership, respectively, from Prairie View A&M University of Texas. Rev. Seymore also earned a Doctor of Philosophy in Organizational Leadership from Northcentral University of Arizona. His dissertation topic was, "The Impact of a Pastor's Education on the Growth of a CME Church."

On local, state, and national levels, Dr. Seymore has used vision, organization, and practicality to train and improve the performance of churches, educational agencies, and other non-profit organizations throughout the country. Dr. Seymore is an experienced organizational development consultant and trainer. In addition to leadership and ministry development work with local ministries, Rev. Seymore has been the featured facilitator for several workshops, regional, and national conferences.

A seasoned educator and public-school administrator, Dr. Seymore has worked in educational organizations and institutions in Texas, Georgia, North Carolina, Maryland, and California. His career aim was to improve the environment where teaching and learning takes place. His educational aim was to use "lessons learned from the trenches" to develop and support current teachers and administrators.

Dr. Seymore is the immediate past Dean of Education at Lincoln University in Jefferson City, Missouri. In addition, Dr. Seymore mentors The Academy for

Men of Color in Education at Lincoln, a program which aims to attract, support, and graduate employable young men with urban school systems throughout the country.

Dr. Seymore is the Dean of Leadership Development and Director of Christian Education for the 3rd Episcopal District of the Christian Methodist Episcopal Church. He is a leadership coach, strategic planning facilitator, and ministry evaluator. Dr. Seymore is the founder of the MoreSey Foundation, featuring the signature program "I've Got Shoulders;" a campaign designed to highlight the narrative of people of color BY people of color.

Dr. Seymore is a member of Kappa Delta Pi, an international honor society for educators; the 100 Black Men of the America; Alpha Phi Alpha Fraternity, Incorporate, and the National Association for the Advancement of Colored People.

Dr. Seymore is a proud father of two adult sons, Marrix II and Johnston Alexander Seymore. He lives by the mission of being an ambassador of vision; uniquely molded to glorify God, equipped to edify His people, and commanded to empower them to further the Kingdom of God. He executes this mission based on Habakkuk 2:2 "*Write the vision and make it plain!*"